BASIC BAIT FISHING

BASIC BAIT FISHING

Ray Ovington

Stackpole Books

Published by
STACKPOLE BOOKS
Cameron and Kelker Streets
P. O. Box 1831
Harrisburg, PA 17105

Cover photograph courtesy of Cy DeCosse Incorporated.
Line drawings of the freshwater species in Part Three courtesy of The Pennsylvania Fish Commission.
Line drawings of the saltwater species in Part Three courtesy of The International Game Fish Association.

Printed in the U.S.A.

Library of Congress Cataloging in Publication Data

Ovington, Ray.
  Basic bait fishing.

  1. Bait fishing. I. Title.
SH455.4.085 1984   799.1'2   83-18058
ISBN 0-8117-2173-6 (pbk.)

Contents

Introduction

You cast a live minnow, impaled on a small hook, into a trout stream's current slick. As the line is fed from the reel through the rod guides, the minnow is carried along in the current and it swirls and sinks down into the pocket of gravel where a hungry trout is waiting for it. In a graceful movement of fins and tail, the trout grabs the minnow, you feel the action, and the fight is on.

A bass, sitting out the warm weather on the bottom of a lake, sees an earthworm drifting by him slowly. It is attached to a small hook on a very thin leader. With no weight to inhibit its natural drifting action, it looks just like a wounded fish drifting naturally in the water. The bass is not hunting for food at the moment; but because it is his nature to investigate anything toothsome that comes along, he rises from his hole, noses the bait, even mouths it a bit, and finally sucks it into his mouth and moves out of his hole. The line straightens out and you feel the action and strike. The bass is hooked: you know it by the sudden jerk and the long run as your rod bends in resistance.

Out on the ocean a bonefish, stripped of its backbone and firmly wound to a large hook, is dragged tantalizingly along the water's surface. Marlin from 150 to 1000 pounds are in the vicinity. They are finicky but voracious feeders, and they can see a bait fish from quite a distance. One marlin spies the bait and follows it briefly while your fishing cruiser holds its pace to keep the bait moving naturally in its wake. The captain has spotted the marlin's dorsal fin cutting the water some yards behind the bait, and you are now in your fighting chair, rod in hand and on the alert. A rush of disturbed water right behind the bait signals the strike, and the line bursts away from the outrigger. You and the marlin are locked fast in a struggle that will last up to an hour.

That's bait fishing—definitely a sporting proposition!

The purpose of this book is to offer helpful information on catching common species of fresh and saltwater fish with natural baits. For those who have never fished before, this book will answer many questions and create new ones. Hopefully, it will give you all the facts needed for success: tackle selection and proper use; fishing rigs and how to make them; all important knots and how to tie them (and when to use them); fishing techniques; the nature of baits; what baits to use on what fish; and much more.

For those who have fished before with artificial lures and flies, I hope that this book presents bait fishing in a new light; namely, being as much of a sporting proposition as fishing with other types of equipment and methods.

For too many years the writers of fishing books have accentuated fishing with artificial lures and flies, their premise being that catching fish this way is more sporting. I beg to differ with them. Any method used that is legal and offers the fish a sporting chance, while offering the highest challenge to the angler's tackle and technique, presents the opportunity for true sportsmanship. The fisherman who kills more fish than he needs or more than the law allows is not a sportsman whether he uses natural baits or artificial ones.

Certainly there is indeed a great deal of fun in catching fish with artificial lures, but bait fishing can be its equal and at many times its superior. I have experienced many days of inaction with artificials. However, many a dull day has turned into a red-letter affair when natural baits were used. Natural conditions dictate natural baits more often than artificial ones. In Florida, for example, in the streams that are dark and deep, the artificial lure never measures up to the natural bait.

Brook trout in Maine rivers and connecting streams will refuse all manner of flies (and even spinners) most of the time, but the minute you impale a red, firm, small worm on a hook and flip it out of the canoe, you'll have several trout vying for it.

No matter what kind of bait or lure you use, the secret of great fishing lies in the correct selection and skillful use of the right gear, baits and lures, taking into account the species to be caught, and the prevailing conditions. No one should assume that just because he chucks a hooked minnow or worm or other form of bait overboard that he will automatically connect with a monster. There's a lot more to it than that, and that is the reason and the need for this book.

If you have never fished before, bait fishing is a great way to begin. You will save a lot of money by using bait rather than artificial lures. Over the years, when teaching beginners the lore of fishing, I have always encouraged them to fish with bait first; they get more action faster and so become hooked along with the rest of us who have been at it for years.

For those who may dabble with lures and fly fishing, travelling the angling path toward becoming the complete angler, bait fishing offers the basics. To the reader who considers himself a seasoned angler but who may have bypassed bait fishing, this book will open new horizons.

In this day and age, the growing number of small boat owners who have craft suitable for fresh and saltwater angling can enjoy bait fishing to its fullest. There is quick access to surf, beach, bay, bayou, and ocean, with bait liveries, marinas and outfitters ready to assist them.

As always, old fashioned luck is always there affecting your results. But there are ways to reduce the risk of coming home empty-handed. These fundamentals and basics are outlined here by one who has learned it all the hard, sometimes fishless, way. Whether you are a seasoned angler or a novice, an old fisherman or a young one, there is much interesting and helpful detail here about all the baits and bait fishing tackle and techniques—all intended to help you along the way. May we meet someday to compare catches.

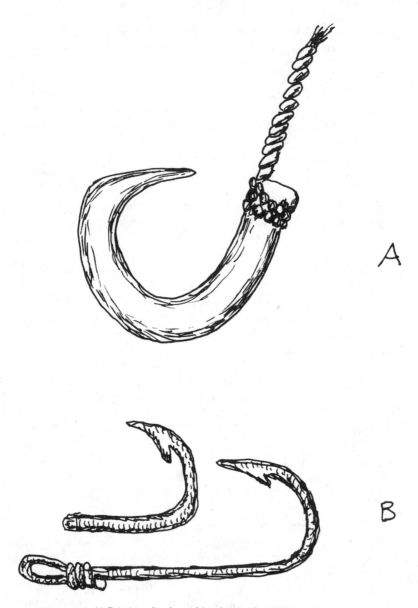

A) Primitive hook used by the Sandwich Islanders.
B) Mycenian fish hook, predating those found in Syria. Used with hand lines from early times.

An old Chinese proverb states that the big fish feed on the medium-size fish; the medium-size fish feed on the small fish; the small fish feed on the tiny fish; and the tiny fish eat mud. Yes, the food chain, when thoroughly understood, is an open book to the angler in search of almost any type of food and game fish when he goes forth with rod and line. His terminal tackle and rigs and his technique are based on what the ancient Chinaman told him long ago.

Throughout the hundreds, even thousands, of years, man (and a few women) have gone forth to catch fish for food and fun. It all began with very crude equipment and techniques. Today, those same basic ways to catch fish have been improved through the miracles of science and space-age technology.

PART ONE

Tackle

BASIC TACKLE

Hundreds of combinations of tackle used on various species of fish under all conditions of fresh and saltwater angling have been developed through the years. There are specific types of tackle. Terminal gear, or the "business end" of the line, includes swivels, sinkers, leaders, hooks, and bait rigs, all of equal importance and many in number and quality.

Choosing the correct combination is not difficult or complicated, but it is most important to select tackle that is easy to handle. Not all people have the same "feel" for fishing gear, any more than they do for tennis racquets, golf clubs, or sports cars. There can be variations in rod weights and lengths, for example, to fulfill the same project. Conditions also enter the picture. If one desires long casts in a trout stream, a certain rig is needed. On the other hand, the same rig may be not at all ideal when fishing in a small brook. Flounder bottom fishing can be done without a rod, while fishing for marlin and sailfish requires a very strong rod and reel with large line capacity.

When the art of casting is involved, the combination of rod, reel, line, leaders, and terminal weights and hooks has to be balanced. Too light a tip action in a rod will not allow casting a heavy weight; too strong a tip action will tend to flip the bait off on the cast.

BALANCED TACKLE

To catch fish with bait or artificial lures, proper tackle is a must. This can consist of very simple inexpensive equipment, or it can be a rig quite involved and costly. Buy and use first-rate tackle. A simple hand line made of store string, a metal bolt or screw, or even a stone for weight, and a penny hook will suffice in simple fishing. But tackle can also involve extremely heavy reels, miles of line, expensive rods, and fighting chairs totaling well over a thousand dollars in cost. The wrong decision can be made in choosing simple tackle as easily as with the most complex, but there is no reason or need to do so if the facts are known.

Fishing tackle was originally designed as a result of man's need to catch fish for food. Sporting gear is merely tackle refined to produce the most action and allow sporting principles to prevail in fishing; it serves to deliver the bait accurately and effortlessly, be it small and light, or big and heavy.

Make friends with your tackle store proprietor and discuss local fishing needs. Talk with experienced anglers; watch them fish and note their tackle and its use. But be prudent in buying: cheap tackle can be an abomination and a waste of money. It is better to buy well-known brand names rather than something that "looks just as good at half the price." Good tackle, well cared for, will last many years and give dependable service.

Extra-heavy line is unnecessary and difficult to cast; extra-light line will break too easily and fail to get the bait to its destination. A heavy weight cannot be cast at all with flimsy rod action. Choose a reel that makes casting as effortless as possible and contains enough line of sufficient strength (pound test).

FLY FISHING TACKLE

Fly fishing tackle is specifically designed to cast very light flies and lures. This tackle is also excellent for bait fishing in both fresh and saltwater. The fly rod looks like the one in the illustration; the reel is behind the hand and, for the most part, functions only to hold the line. Except with very big fish in fast water, the fish is seldom "played" from the reel: the line control is manipulated by hand in harmony with the bend of the rod. In spinning and bait casting, the fish is played from the reel and the cast lure is controlled directly by the action of the reel.

Rods are made in two- or three-piece sections. Bamboo was the most practical material before the advent of fiberglass and modern plastics. Fly reels are of single action, meaning there is no "gearing up" as in bait casting or spinning reels. One turn of the handle means one turn of the spool. Some fly reels have line drags or "brakes" that are adjustable for pressure and line control as well as for playing the fish (such as, in the case of big game fish, the fly reels used for bonefish, salmon, and the like).

Lines are designed in three styles: level, double-tapered, and "shoot casting." The latter is seldom used in bait fishing. The most practical line for our purposes here is the level line (either floating or sinking) for close-in work or, at the most, a double-tapered line, usually made of braided nylon, for casting extremely light weights long distances.

Tackle must be balanced. The reel must not be too heavy, the line neither too light nor too heavy. The accompanying chart shows the selection of balanced fly tackle for both fresh and saltwater fishing.

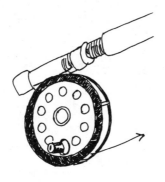

RECOMMENDED TACKLE FOR FLY FISHING

FISH SIZE AND CONDITIONS	ROD LENGTH	ROD ACTION	LINE SIZE	AFTMA	REEL SIZE
Small trout, panfish, small streams, ponds.	6 1/2'	Dry Fly Medium	C-HCH, HCF	6	Small
	(Short, lightweight, used only for very small, light baits, short casts.)				
Same, with bigger fish.	8 1/2'	Medium	B-GBG-GBF	7	Medium
Longer casts, heavier baits.	8 1/2'	Dry Fly	B-GBG-GBF	7	Medium
	(Good for bait fishing fast streams because of a little more backbone and power when using heavier baits for fighting fish in strong currents.)				
Long distance, heavy baits, fresh and salt-water fishing.	9'	Bass Bug	GAF	8	Heavy Large Cap.
	(Considered the bass bugging rod, it is well adapted to bait fishing for every fresh and saltwater species, including bonefish and tarpon.)				
Long distance, heavy winds, big baits, big fish.	9 1/2 to 10'	Heavy	G3AF	10	Heavy Large Cap.
	(Anything up to muskellunge, tarpon.)				

SPINNING TACKLE

Properly set up and used, the spinning outfit is by far the most versatile combination of rod, reel, and line, and it is used extensively in casting and trolling baits for both fresh and saltwater fishing. The ultralight spinning combinations can be used for small trout and panfish baits, the medium freshwater weights are adequate for most species including pike and musky. These last require heavier rods, stiffer actions, and heavier lines. They are also excellent for salt-water species up to and including the sailfish, so one rig can be used interchangeably. Most medium weight spinning gear can be used in both waters for comparable fish.

Rod and reel are assembled as in the illustration with the reel (open-faced type) hanging down in the center of the rod handle, and closed-face reels are used above or below as shown. The line guides are bigger than on the fly or bait casting rods because the line comes off the end of the reel spool in coils. The handle is equipped with an antireverse gear so it will not spin around, but will activate the adjustable drag. The rods are generally two-piece and preferably glass. The preferred line is monofilament nylon; it can vary in weight from one-pound to forty-pound test. Rods extend from four to nine feet as in the case of big surf casting tips.

The advantage of spinning gear is that it enables the angler to

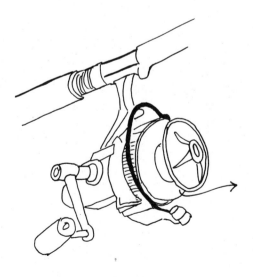

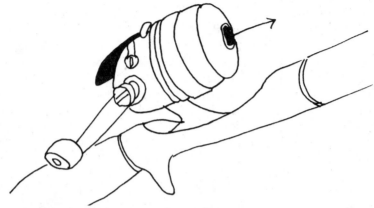

cast extremely lightweight baits great distances when the tackle is balanced. There is no danger of backlash or reel line tangle due to overspinning of the reel spool as frequently happens with conventional bait casting reels. The spinning spool is stationary; the line is pulled over the end as needed rather than over the revolving bale.

Again, balance is necessary for the project at hand. To cast an unweighted worm in a small stream requires a light, soft-action rod and light line. To fling a dead shrimp far into the surf requires a heavy rod, a big reel with large line capacity, and a heavy line and sinker rig. The accompanying chart can be a useful reference and guide.

BAIT CASTING TACKLE

Bait casting gear was designed 100 years ago as a simple crank, spool, pole, and line. It has been refined a good deal since and has become the most popular casting outfit for both artificial lure use and bait casting—especially in cases of freshwater bass, pike, and trout. It was basically refined in rod types for trolling, casting, and, particularly, surf long-distance casting. Its advocates swear by it to this day despite the advent of spinning gear and, although it diminished in popularity for a time, it's currently regaining its proper place on the fishing scene.

The bait casting reel is mounted above the handle and the rod is either one- or two-piece, joining at the handle, or butt section,

RECOMMENDED TACKLE FOR SPINNING

FISH SIZE AND CONDITIONS	ROD LENGTH	ROD ACTION	LINE TEST	LURE WEIGHT	REEL SIZE
Panfish, small trout, quiet waters.	6'	U/LT	2–6 lbs.	1/16 to 1/4 oz.	Ultra Light
(Designed for catching smallest game and panfish, yet capable of handling bigger ones in open water. Very sporting.)					
Small fish, fresh and saltwater.	6 1/2'	LT	2–6 lbs.	1/8 to 3/8 oz.	Small
(A bit larger than above for heavier baits, longer casts and tidal or stream currents.)					
Bass, pike, small tarpon, sea trout.	7 1/2'	SE	4–12 lbs.	1/4 to 3/4 oz.	Small Medium Cap.
(Conventional level-wind reels can also be used and are preferred by steelheaders and big-fish anglers of the South.)					
Striped bass, pike, musky, med. saltwater fish.	7'9"	MED	10–30 lbs.	1 to 3 oz.	Medium
(A standard two-handed rod for light saltwater and heavy steelhead baiting, live shrimp popping, up to big tarpon.)					
Surf, most big lakes, big freshwater fish, med. saltwater fish.	9'	MED	10–25 lbs.	1 to 3 oz.	Medium Large Cap.
(The surfer's favorite, also for jetty fishing; also used for cod, pollock, grouper, sea bass, cobia, amberjack, with heavy sinkers and terminal gear.)					

Legend:

U/LT	Ultra-light	V/HVY	Very heavy	UFT	Ultra-fast taper
LT	Light	MED	Medium	FT	Fast taper
LTM	Light-medium	HVY	Heavy	SE	Salmon egg

and tip. The reel is the multiplying type: four turns of the spool to one turn of the handle for quick line retrieve. A level-wind bar travels back and forth across the reel spool to distribute the line evenly for the next cast. There are two types of controls for drag: the star or the button. Line is generally of braided nylon, though some anglers use the monofilament line with equal zeal.

Balance is the key here. For bait fishing, a softer tip on a longer rod is required; a shorter, stiffer-tipped rod is generally used for throwing heavy artificial lures. A shorter tip can be used for trolling as well as casting, though it is frequently better for trolling. The saltwater boat rod is a variation of the typical freshwater trolling rod. The surf rod, a big double-handed rod with a long tip, is used for distance casting from beach, jetty, or boat. Several combinations are shown in the accompanying charts for this most versatile fishing set-up. Choose tackle for the job at hand.

These recommendations should be checked out in the light of local conditions at a local tackle store where you can discuss your personal bait fishing needs with competent tackle salesmen—men who fish themselves and talk reality rather than sales pitches and theory. Look over the tackle. Get the feel of the rod actions and become acquainted with the reels and lines. Then it will be time to consider the terminal tackle for the particular bait fishing to be done locally. If planning an extended trip to an area where availability of tackle and terminal gear is bound to be scant or nonexistent, better bring along a large assortment, and include a good brand of lubricating oil. Reels should be taken apart at home so they can be put back together again after an "on-the-spot" cleaning at the fishing camp. Make sure rods are safely packed in tubular containers. Before putting the line on the reel, read and reread the instructions carefully. Tackle dealers should demonstrate how to wind the reel or, quite literally, do it for their customers on their line winders.

RECOMMENDED TACKLE FOR BAIT CASTING

FISH SIZE AND CONDITIONS	ROD LENGTH	ROD ACTION	LINE SIZE	LURE WEIGHT	REEL SIZE
Light fresh and saltwater fish.	6 1/2'	LT	4–10 lbs.	1/8 to 3/8 oz.	Medium Spin or Bait casting
	(Rod should have ultra-fast taper to handle a wide margin of lure weights. The light tip will cast light weights and the change to heavier line will allow the tip to handle the heavies.)				
Light fresh and saltwater fish.	6 1/2'	MED/LT	8–15 lbs.	3/8 to 5/8 oz.	Medium Spin or Bait casting
	(This in medium and fast taper is good for bass, walleye and pike, bone–fish, permit and small tarpon, using heavy jigs and bait or sinkers and bait.)				
Medium saltwater and heavy freshwater fish.	5 1/2'	MED/UFT	10–20 lbs.	3/8 to 1 oz.	Medium Bait casting
	(For rugged freshwater fishing as well as boat, bay and beach saltwater work, particularly trolling and heavy baiting. A rod built to stop fish such as snook from hanging in the mangroves or big striped bass.)				
Casting and trolling heavy weights deep.	5 1/2'	V/HVY	17 to 50 lbs.	1 3/4 to 6 oz.	Medium Saltwater
	(For muskellunge, lake trout, snook, tarpon and even dolphin, 'cuda and the like, if you don't try to kill too fast.)				
Trolling, jetty or heavy bottom fishing.	5 1/2'	V/HVY	17 to 50 lbs.	1 to 2 1/2 oz.	Medium Saltwater
	(Similar to above but preferred by bottom sinker bouncers as an all-purpose deep-trolling and big-fish rig up to school tuna.)				
Trolling, bottom fishing.	5 1/2'	LT	20 to 40 lbs.	2 1/2 to 4 oz.	Large Saltwater
	(Light bay and deep lake fishing with wire lines.)				
	(Legend: As in preceding recommended tackle table.)				

When assembling a rod, align the line leader guides before inserting the section into its ferrule joint. Do not twist or bend the rod while inserting or removing. If a line becomes snagged while fishing, do not strain the rod to get it free. Pull in the line directly: better to break a line and/or lose a rig than to damage a rod.

SALTWATER GEAR

Basic saltwater bait fishing rods, reels, and terminal tackle are divided into overlapping categories: bottom fishing/trolling; general, all-purpose casting; and strictly distance casting rods. The rig can be either a conventional bait casting or spinning type. Their functions and requirements are similar, and both do the job.

For freshwater trolling and still fishing, the general, all-purpose medium weight rigs will suffice for small fish species; but where

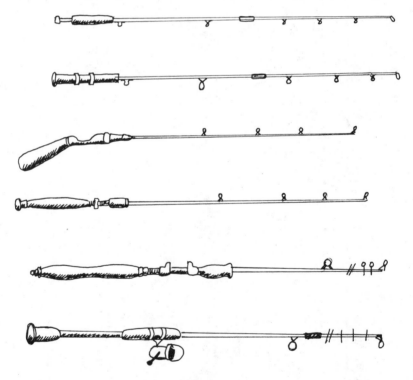

greater weights, depths of water, and heftier sinkers are encountered, heavier tackle is required. While it is possible to use one rod and reel for all these purposes (particularly the spinning rod), it is better to fit the tackle closer to the task at hand.

The typical boat rod used for bottom bait fishing is not required to cast the bait any distance. Rod action need not be, nor should it be, too soft. In order to control bait at great depths, hook the fish on the first nibble and keep it from snagging bottom rocks and debris. You must respond to the slightest pull. When after big fish such as those found in extremely deep offshore waters and near shipwrecks, use a stouter rod with a large capacity reel and proportionately heavier line.

Casting rods are a different proposition. For the bait fisherman using a heavy sinker for distance, a fairly stiff-tipped rod is needed whether he is casting from a boat, jetty, point of rocks, or the beach.

ASSEMBLING AND HANDLING THE TACKLE

For boat fishing, trolling, or bottom baiting for trout, bass, and lake trout, or fishing in the bay for porgies, flounders, small grouper, southern sea trout, (possibly) striped bass, snook, and similar species, use a boat rod of medium weight and length. Attach a saltwater reel of correct line capacity filled with the proper line. Terminal rigging has been preselected for the type of fish and kind of bait.

The reel drag should be set at a point a few ounces under the line's breaking point so the line will pull off the reel before it breaks, thus avoiding excessive strain on the rod. Practice with the combination by tying the line to something stationary. In this way the line's breaking limits can readily be discovered. Set the reel handle on antireverse so the handle will not spin on strike. For bottom fishing, merely drop the terminal tackle overboard and allow it to touch the bottom. Quickly reel in a foot or more, lifting the bait and sinkers off the bottom. It is best to hold the rod in both hands and be ready for a strike. One can also give some action to the bait by lifting the rod up and down rhythmically. For trolling, set the rod in a rod holder if there is one on the boat, but watch it! Be careful not to allow your fingers near the reel and never grab hold of the line on a strike: it can cut right through to the bone if the fish is big.

CASTING

Proper tackle set-up requires the line test again be taken into consideration. In addition, the bait casting reel is adjusted for spool revolutions which ultimately control the line in casting. Some anglers prefer the spool to be free and fast; others like it controlled a bit to avoid backlash, especially when casting very light weights. The spin caster need not worry, for the line will come off the reel in direct relation to the pressure of the cast.

To effect the easiest and most effortless cast, select the tackle to fit the need of the moment. Actual techniques of casting and retrieving are described later after considering the various terminal tackle rigs most often used.

Most fly reels of the lighter variety do not have drag adjustments, but those that do can be set to accommodate a hard pull on the line by either fish or fisherman and will not allow a tangle due to overspin. The angler draws off the line by hand, so there is no required setting of the reel drag except as mentioned before in the case of big fighting fish circumstances, such as bonefish and Atlantic salmon—all played from the reel.

There are no controls on most simple fly reels, so it is best to test the line strength. Attach the end of the leader to a stationary object and strain the rod and line to nearly the breaking point. Due to the spring of the long fly rod, much of the direct strain on the line is absorbed. It is surprising how much pressure can be applied before reaching the danger point for either rod or line.

FISHING LINE SELECTION

During the past thirty years we have gone from fishing "cord" to synthetic material lines. They have greatly increased the tensile strength of fishing lines, eliminated the unevenness of test of the fiber lines, and eliminated much of the care needed to keep lines up to their expected strength and stretch capabilities.

Monofilament nylon is the basis of all synthetic lines. It is made in single strands of various strengths and diameters; braided monofilament lines are made from these strands. Actual monofilament is the all-purpose line for modern fishing, and it should be used for

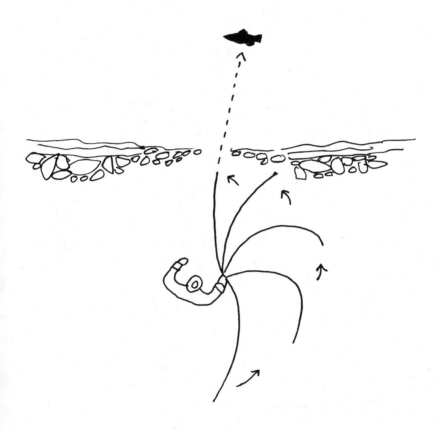

Note that the cast is made in the sidewinder fashion whether it be with spinning, fly, or bait casting rods. The overhead cast can be used with very light and tightly hooked baits, but most anglers prefer to "swing it out" to the fish sideways. This requires a lot more timing of the cast, in order to avoid whipping the bait off with too fast a cast, or dropping it down to the water or sand with too slow a cast. Also, the timing of the line release in relation to the direction of the cast must be controlled and directed.

all spinning reels regardless of size. It is also used almost exclusively for plug and lure casting, ocean trolling, and all saltwater fishing in general. Monofilament is also used in the making of tapered leaders for fly rod fishing.

There are many different brands available with specific qualities to suit almost any need. Some lines are soft and stretch more than others, and some are stiff. Softer lines are better in freshwater fishing since they have to be tied into knots for attachment to hooks and leaders. But softness alone is not always the answer to your needs: leaders that are too soft tend to weaken more quickly than stiffer ones. Many saltwater anglers like a middle-of-the-road stiffness/softness ratio, particularly where line abrasion is a factor.

Braided dacron line is used for saltwater trolling rather than braided nylon since it is thinner in diameter and offers less stretch.

The bottom line on which to base your selection is of course the pound test as given by the manufacturer. Quite often, for its own security, the manufacturer lists the line test below the actual strength of the line. This can be very important to the angler out after a record fish, since these records are based on the actual test of the line used.

Fly fishing lines come in braided nylon and braided dacron and the choice is sometimes hard to make between the actual advantages of one over the other. Most rod makers suggest certain lines to conform to the actions of their rods and these should be followed for the best balance. The strength of the actual line is not important, since leaders of far less pound test are used between the fly line and the lure or bait hook attached at the end.

KNOTS AND BASIC WIRE WRAPS

Tying a secure and positive knot in monofilament is a much different problem from tying such a knot in one of the old-fashioned materials such as silk, for example. Many of the classical knots are not as suitable as those that have been devised by noted anglers in recent years for specific use with nylon line. Many of the old knots severely reduce the actual breaking point of the line since they tend to flatten and squeeze the line, thus weakening it. Also, the properties of the nylon and even the braided nylon require an entirely different concept in knot tying.

The most dangerous pressure on any knot is a sudden snaplike pull. While the line will stretch to a point, the strength of the knot is, in the last analysis, the determining factor between a broken line and a sustained pull to get the fish in. Therefore, it is wise to remember to retie any knots, particularly after a tough battle with a fish or a stretching contest with a snag. It is much better to try to extricate the hook from a snag by reaching down to the hook itself to remove it rather than to try to pull it loose, thereby stretching and weakening the line and binding the knot too tight. A knot that has had this treatment will likely break quicker than one that has not.

Always select a knot suited to your purpose. Shown later is a selection of such knots and how to tie them. Don't just tie any old knot even though you might be in a hurry. A fish lost by the use of the wrong knot will not reach home for baking. Don't ad lib with your own ideas unless you are prepared for extensive testing. This does not mean that all the best knots have been invented, but until you can come up with something better by proof, stick to the ones shown here.

Another precaution in tying is to draw the knot tight, slowly, making sure that the various curves and twists are lined up and in order as the knot takes its final shape. Again, don't be in a hurry. Tie down that knot and secure it properly. Then you can test it for its strength and slippage by pulling the line sharply: if the knot has come to rest properly it will not break off or slip. If you have to retie, use a fresh length of line. Never try to tie a line that has been squeezed, grooved, or misshapened in any way. Light lines and leaders can easily be drawn to perfection by hand, but, when tying knots with heavier line, a pliers gripped to the hook, not the line, is necessary to pull on the knot to tighten.

It takes an experienced fisherman to develop knots that will really work, and even those knots are eventually improved upon. When nylon monofilament first came on the market, the instruction folder enclosed with the product showed several traditional knots that would be correct with the material. These have been improved upon by anglers all over the world. Experienced guides in the Florida Keys, for example, have devised their own specialities, as have guides in the Great Lakes and the streams of the Northeast.

The first knot shown in the series was demonstrated to me by

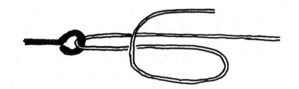

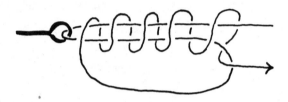

Once you have learned to tie the first knot in this series, you will have mastered the basics for future knots. As shown in the diagram, take several inches of line and run it through the eye so you will have enough line to work with easily. Now turn the end back toward the hook eye to form a circle. Grasp both strands of line and the crossing strand in a single grip with the thumb and forefinger. Next you form six turns around both strands of line and then pull through the circle as shown in diagram 2. Still holding the line in your thumb and forefinger, pull the end of the line in the direction indicated making sure all of the wraps are lined up and tighten correctly. This will insure an even pressure and tight knot and will give you a strong connection. To finish the knot, simply slide the knot tightly against the hook eye.

Diagram 3 shows the completed knot ready to be slipped up to the hook eye. Diagram 4 shows the knot pushed up to the hook eye. If you desire to leave a little slack line for free movement of the hook or lure, simply place a match stick between the hook eye and the approaching knot and then tighten the line. The knot will "set" away from the hook, allowing it to swing freely and not bind.

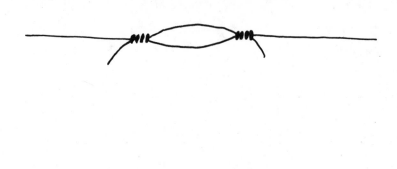

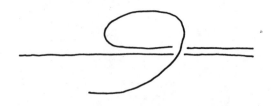

To tie the line-to-line knot, you use the same basic knot; but in this case you are tying two different strands together. The parallel strands are merely two different lines rather than the single strand.

Form the knot circle with line A around line B, making the six wrap arounds and then pulling the line end down and back as shown in diagram 2. Diagram 3 shows one half of the knot completed. You simply duplicate the first knot on the other side now and you end up with what is shown in diagram 4. These two knots are then slid carefully and evenly together to form a tight bond.

If you desire to leave one of the line ends as a tippet for an additional hook, sinker or bobber, start tying with a long extra end—say about 8 inches long.

This knot can also be used for tying line to leader if the diameter of both lines is fairly similar.

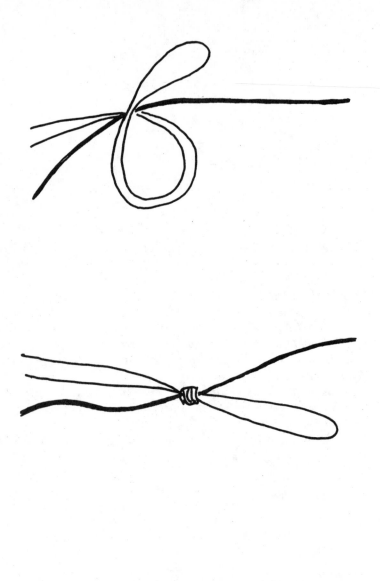

While this line-to-leader knot looks more complicated, it really isn't. First you begin as usual, doubling back several inches of line, and then overlap the doubled part of the line with the end of the heavy leader to begin the first wrapping step of the basic knot. Take the doubled end around the strands and through the circle with the loop. Make three passes only. Hold the strands with the left hand while slipping a finger in the loop. Now pull the loop so that the knot begins to tighten up, watching it as you go to make sure all is even and the knot becomes snug and then tight.

The next step is to turn the lines around and tie another complete knot, running the heavy leader around both strands of line. Make your three turns and then pull gently, bringing the knot down snug.

Slide the two knots together by using an opposing pull on the main leader and both strands of line. Continue until the rig is snug and then tight.

To snell a hook with either line or leader material, even light wire, you can use the same basic knot as shown in the diagram. First slip the line through the eye of the hook with an end of at least six inches for easy tying. Form the usual knot and keep it tight against the hook shank by using your thumb and forefinger. Several turns can be then made over the hook shank and also through the circle. Pull it all together by holding the end of the line in one hand and the hook shank in the other. Pull gently, setting the knot properly, and there you have it.

This is also a very good way to tie on spinners, weights and lures.

The improved clinch knot is an oldie that is still used for attaching hooks, bait rigs, spinners, and weights to the line. It is quick and easy and a very secure knot.

Thread the line through the hook eye, keeping several inches of line to tie with ease. Next, wrap five or six turns around the basic line and, while holding the lines together, bring the line end around to the top of the knot at the hook and slip it through the space ahead of the hook eye and between the wraps and the outside loop. While holding onto the folds, tighten by pulling the main line until the wraps fold together evenly and snugly. When tying on a heavy spoon or plug or other weighty object, you can merely thread the line through the eye, drop the weight and spin it a few times, and then complete the knot in a matter of seconds.

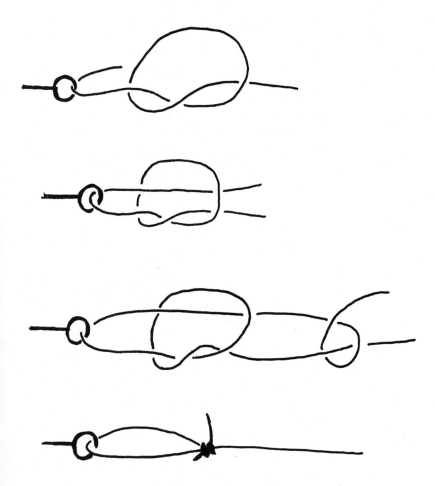

What is called the end loop knot is one of the simplest to tie and a very effective knot for a lot of uses. It also affords you measured freedom of the lure to swing within the confines of the loop at the end of the knot so that the lure will be able to act naturally and not be bound stiffly, an advantage when using very heavy line or monofilament. Merely slip the end of the line through the eye, saving enough to work with easily and behind this form a simple square knot. Send the line end through the center of the loop of the square knot and out beyond make a half hitch. Tighten at the desired loop size or snug the knot up tight as you prefer.

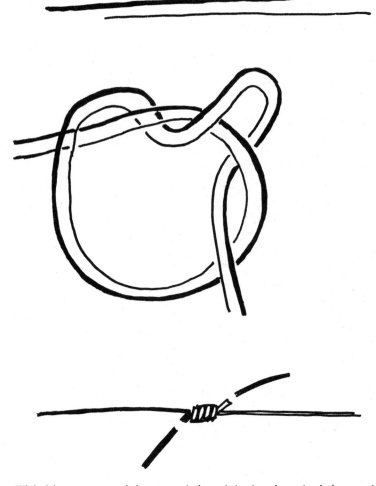

    While I have never used the surgeon's knot, it is given here simply because it is a well accepted knot for tying two lengths of line together, or two pieces of leader material, or one of each kind as the case may be. It is also used when it is desired to have a tippet extend from the finished knot for the use of a side leader for adding lures, weights, bait hooks, or even a bobber to the basic line.

    Place the two strands of line side by side and form a simple square knot. Then at the end, while holding the entire knot in the fingers, run the end of the line back through the wide loop. At first tie this knot with a lot of slack and a wide circle just to get to learn the steps, and then you can tighten up. The trick here is to be able to pull the strands together evenly so that the knot will not be uneven when it is drawn together for its final stage.

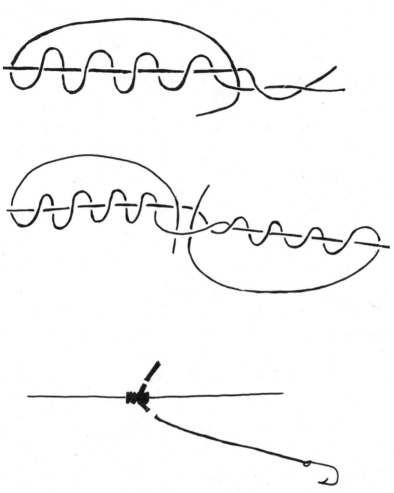

The blood knot has many uses—for tying two strands of leader or line material together. It is the old standby for those who make tapered leaders for fly fishing and is also used when one or two extended tippets are wanted for the addition of corks, weights, extra flies, or hooks.

At first you feel as though you have two cats by the tail, but a few tries and you'll have it down pat. Start out by overlapping both sections of line, and firm the first twist and loop to complete part one of the knot. Then, holding the untightened section of the knot in one hand, you duplicate the same routine in the other hand in the other direction. Make sure that the line ends come out of the center hole in opposite directions. Tighten by pulling the knots slowly together by holding one end of the line in your teeth and holding the two separate sections of the knots in your other hand. You can tie leader material as fine as 7× with this knot and it will retain the strength to an amazing degree—just so long as you pull evenly without scarring the leader material as you go.

a surf fisherman who catches more fish than anyone I know in Florida. He learned it from Vic Dunaway, a well-known sportsman and fishing expert of the Southland. It is called the uniknot system and produces a knot that is most versatile. Vic claims the knot's strength is almost 100%. It holds up under sudden pressure and even a snap-like pull. It can be used in many situations.

You will need a knot to tie the butt end of your line so that it will slip tightly onto the spool when you are loading your reel. You will then need a knot to tie line to line in case of a breakage. One joins the line to the leader, and another allows the use of a branch leader or tippet (as used in fly fishing) and additional weights (as used in bait fishing). A tapered leader needs a leader to leader knot. And finally you get down to the knot used to attach a swivel, lure, weight, or hook to the leader end. All of these knots can be made from the first knot in the series as shown. There are alternates to these that are also shown for your choice.

Take some time off. Study the diagrams and captions here and learn to tie these knots with your eyes closed. You may have to tie one in the dark or in a hurry.

WIRE LEADER WRAPPING

An art in itself, the making of wire leaders and attaching them to terminal tackle has come a long way since the early days. The wire material has been manufactured to meet specific needs, and its selection is as important as the ways in which you twist and tie it for maximum safety, strength, and holding power. Tying wire wraps requires as much or more care as tying leaders made of nylon.

Wire leaders are used mainly by Pacific salmon and big game fishermen who troll the ocean surfaces and depths. They are also used in the Great Lakes and in some cases for fishing for pike and musky. The wire leader is used for fish that have strong, sharp teeth or for those that are particularly heavy.

There are several types of wire for general angling use today. The most common is the stainless steel single strand leader wire in various diameters and pound tests. Then there is the Monel single strand trolling wire which is actually a wire line. Wire cable is twisted wire filaments used mainly for leaders and there is also a wire cable coated with plastic for leaders. If you are tying with single strand wire, all diameters are wrapped in a similar way. The larger the diameter, the more complicated it is to wrap evenly and properly. The use of pliers is strongly recommended. Have cutting pliers, of course, and when you are cutting from the wire spool be careful not to twist the wire as it comes off: keep it straight and uncurled. While working on one end, it is advisable to attach the other end to a solid object until that end is needed to work on. The cutting pliers is also used to give a clean edge to the cut and to bend the cut down so that it will not tear your hand or gather weed and slime when used in the water. Wire specifications are listed later for your selection.

MONOFILAMENT LEADERS AND RIGS

Leaders are the all-important connection between the line that comes from the reel to the business end, the baits and sinkers. The reason for a leader is to allow a quick change of leader and terminal rig from the basic fishing line. A low visibility factor is also important, mainly in most freshwater fishing. The ultimate use is in fly fishing with extremely light and long leaders whether flies or baits are used. The perfect leader would be invisible, yet strong enough to fight the fish, and also strong enough to resist sharp teeth. Obviously there has to be a compromise, and even the best leaders are compromises. Quite often fish become leader shy, especially freshwater trout and bass. But sailfish, and even marlin, can spot a leader ahead of a trolled bait. Quite often, even in deep down fishing, the leader, if it shines at all or inhibits the bait from its natural movement, will spook fish away.

When it comes to the choice between monofilament or wire, monofilament is preferred because of its lower visibility factor. In all cases where fish with teeth that cut are being sought, wire at the hook is needed. Some species of fish such as sea trout, grouper, or snapper have quite effective teeth, but their teeth are not designed to shear a leader, a wire, or a hook. The shark, however, has bony jaws that can severely threaten a nylon leader, unless the fish is very small. The experienced angler would rather try heavier monofilament rather than resort to wire. Nylon can twist, but wire can easily kink and weaken, so care must be used with both. Surf fishermen, especially when working rock and gravel, prefer wire leaders. So do most dock, jetty, and pier anglers.

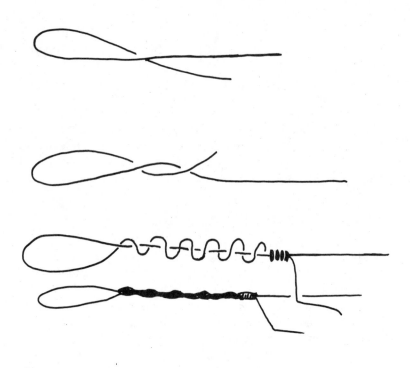

In wrapping wire leaders you must be careful to use smooth pliers and try to avoid scarring the wire or flattening it. This will make your leaders even and easy to handle with the hands and fingers. They will be less likely to pick up weeds and slime if they are free of scars. Some cover the pliers with tape to avoid the cutting edges. Of course, many of these ties can be made by hand unless very heavy material is being used.

The simple haywire twist knot loop is a basic wrap and is used for myriad purposes. Tied just as is shown in the diagram in three stages, it is made by allowing a medium to large loop. The size of the loop is determined by the use to which it will be put. You can always make the loop smaller or larger by merely twisting the loop end or untwisting as the need arises. As in all these wraps, make sure the very end of the wire is tucked under and the end is down so that no sharp point extends out from the main line to catch you or the grass.

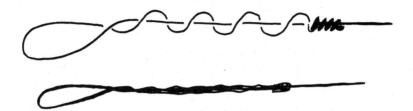

The so-called overhand wire wrap is similar to the preceding wrap with the exception of the method used in tying it off at the bottom. Instead of merely clipping the wire at the end of the wraps, the wraps are made together with the very end of the wire filed off smoothly.

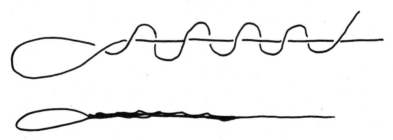

The quick change wire wrap is just what its name implies—a quick way to wrap a sinker, lure, or hook to the wire leader when you are in a hurry! But notice that the wraps are wider than in the preceding knots. This is done for a quick unwrap when it is desired to change the lure quickly and often. You can wrap and unwrap the average wire leader a few times. When you see that the end section is becoming frayed or very uneven, it is likely to become weaker. Cut off the end section you have been using and start again with a fresh section of wire for the next wraps.

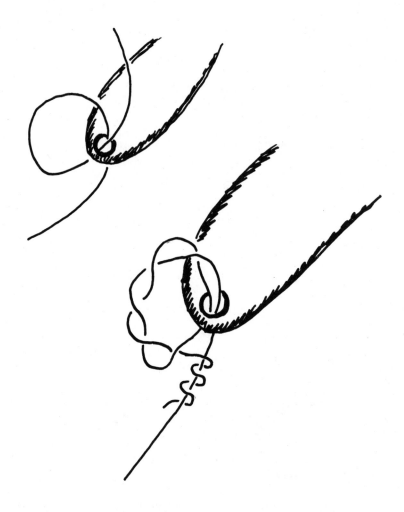

The special spoon wrap is used by anglers attaching a heavy spoon to the leader, or a large bait hook, for that matter. It is a little more involved than the preceding wraps, but it is a secure one, especially when the ultimate in lure freedom is needed.

Wrapped as shown, the wire is double-fed into the spoon hole and then merely wrapped around itself back to the main line of wire and then finally wrapped close with the end filed off.

Single strand wire or braided wire can be instantly tied into a loop by the use of the sleeve and crimper method. It does require a crimping tool (pliers), which can be kept in the tackle box for instant use. The actual sleeves are made in various sizes to fit the general diameter of the wire to be used. Most of the time you will make up this kind of leader on shore, but it can be done in a hurry when needed while you are fishing. It is solid when done perfectly and, even though it looks less safe than wrapping, it is difficult to wrap braided wire, so the crimping method is preferred. The single and double sleeve rigs are shown here.

Here we have the circle wrap as shown previously. It is crimped twice, with wraps in between. You can't be more secure than this.

One of the oldest knots in the history of fishing is the figure eight knot, which is used to attach a hook, ringed sinker, or even a bobber to the line or leader. It can be used with light wire also.

Insert the line through the hook eye and bring it back and over the main line and around and under and then through the loop next to the hook eye. Bring it up close to the eye and tighten gradually, being sure that the folds take a comfortable shape for security.

Leader Connection and Length

Generally, the monofilament leader should be connected to your basic line by a knot such as the surgeon's knot or Albright special knot. These are the most secure ways and ones which offer less chance of picking up slime. They are also easy on the hands when it comes to landing a fish. Some anglers who use combinations of terminal tackle that would tend to twist the line, even if it were armed with trolling or casting fins, attach the leader to a swivel, and the swivel to the line, to avoid twisting the basic fishing line.

In any case, the shortest leader to be used must be at least two feet long. This allows a few inches to be reeled inside the tip guide

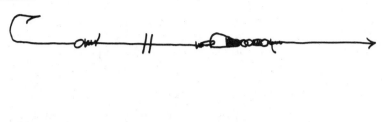

The regulation and standard offshore leader of wire is very simply attached to the running line, either braided or mono, by tying the line into a combination of swivel and snap. The leader length is generally long, leading to the terminal hook. This makes the rig instantly changeable. First you form a double line leading to the swivel, using the conventional knot (fig. 1). This is formed after threading the line through the ring of the swivel.

The wire leader is made by forming a small loop on one end using the haywire twist knot and attaching the hook or lure at the other end of the wire leader, using again, the haywire twist. Consult the table of popular sizes and relationships between wire leader and line. It is suggested that you make up several spare rigs of this type and when the one you are using becomes twisted or bent, take it off and start with the new leader that is kink free. To keep them free of each other and out of the way, find a location on the boat or tackle area where they can be folded in loops and set on hooks or pegs for easy reach.

The short wire leader is also shown for comparison. Both can be tied with only the swivel rather than the snap swivel.

when casting. The leader bears the strain of the friction of the cast and takes the wear instead of the basic line. The leader can be replaced after extended casting periods. By feeling the leader with your fingers you can readily tell when it is becoming flattened, scarred, or weakened.

Much longer leaders are needed for surf casting and ocean casting. The leader should be strong enough to go through the rod guides under terrific pressures. Experienced anglers after mackerel, bluefish, or striped bass use what is termed a shock leader—30 or 40 pound test monofilament added to the line in combination with a short length of wire (say 15 to 20 inches), using a small swivel between the two to avoid spinning in the air on cast or in trolling and retrieving.

You will find many advantages to the shock leader. It often will act as a shock absorber, and it will discourage fish from wrapping up in the leader and breaking the line. Sharks do this! It also fights back at coral, oysters, and discarded automobile parts.

LEADERS FOR FLY AND SPIN FISHING

There is no need to taper a leader that is merely used for the bait hook and bait on any of the standard bait fishing rigs. The only advantage of a tapered leader would be in the case of a hangup. If the hook became caught in a rock or snag and you were to pull against it, the lighter leader would break and you would not lose the entire set-up.

But for fly rod casting, a tapered leader is most often necessary in order to flick that bait, fly, or lure well out there where you want it to go. A balance is needed between the actual fly line and the bait or lure on the end. When the cast is made (the conventional fore and aft cast), the line and leader and lure or bait must form a bow in the air behind you as well as out front where the cast will be laid down on the water. A tapered leader will help this to happen.

In order to arrive at a balanced set-up, the casting arm of the angler, his personality, his rod action—quick, fast, slow, easy— must be taken into consideration. Then the diameter of the end of the line must in some way measure closely with the top section of the leader. Generally, fly line is much more limp than heavy monofilament, so the tricky balance here is to select a butt section of leader to fit the line, and then begin the taper in sections down to the finest point needed for the specific bait or lure to be cast out. If the angler is using any kind of float or sinker on the line, the taper will not help much, since the added weight destroys the bow in the cast and necessitates casts of short length. When the line and leader will be weight free, however, the tapered leader will do its duty well.

The surgeon's knot or the blood knot (latter preferred) is used to tie the leader sections together. For most purposes, it is a good plan to attach a permanent section of monofilament leader to the end of the fly line. This is done with about a three-foot length and is tied in using the uniknot or fast nail knot. Since this connection is strained in casting, it is a good idea to inspect it regularly for wear, especially if it is to go through the tip top guide of the rod regularly. When possible, do not reel the joint into the rod tip guide, even if the leader is longer than the rod.

The basic and most simple tie is that of attaching the lure or hook directly to the running line from the reel. Use either the surgeon's knot or the improved clinch knot for this purpose. This tie is only used when fishing for species that will not readily bite off the leader. The knot has to be set well because, if there is any abnormality in the tie, the knot will break quickly under pressures far below the test of the leader material.

For species of fish that have teeth of any kind, a stouter leader of short length from the lure to the running line is suggested. This can be tied in with any of the standard knots shown. I suggest tying the leader to the line with the blood knot and the lure to the end of the leader with the improved clinch knot.

Shown here are several sample rigs for you to experiment with in arriving at a compatible combination. Your rig should cast well with your specific types of bait and bait weights in conjunction with your line, rod length, and action. Experiment while at home and make a note of the leader lengths and sizes you will want when on

This lure is tied onto the running line from the reel using the double line loop, square-knotted at the hook as shown. For a heavier leader, especially when the lure will be used on or near the bottom or along rocks and snags, a heavier section is tied into the running line with the blood knot.

In order to make sure that the lure does not twist when used in a fast current or tide rip, or when it is being trolled, you can use either a single swivel or a snap swivel for easy lure change.

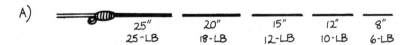

A)

25"	20"	15"	12"	8"
25-LB	18-LB	12-LB	10-LB	6-LB

B)

30"	22"	12"	12"
25-LB	18-LB	10-LB	4-LB

C)

36"	30"	15"	20"
30-LB	20-LB	15-LB	12-LB

D)

72"	24"	14"
35-LB	15-LB	20-LB

Shown here are four tapered leaders with sections tied together with the blood knot. These specifications are only approximations, since the actual leader that suits you will have to be found by experimentation, since there are so many variables of rod action, line weight, cast distance required, lure weight, and water and wind conditions. Try these for size and then experiment on your own to find the perfect leader for your purposes and needs.

A) Average weight trout fly leader (can also be used in light bait fishing).

B) Combination bass and panfish leader for use with small baits, small popping plugs, and tiny spoons and spinners.

C) The big time bass or saltwater game fish leader for large flies and bugs, light baits and lighter spoons, or spinner and bait combinations.

D) The heavyweight saltwater leader: also used in fly fishing for Atlantic salmon, Pacific salmon, muskellunge, and pike, plus of course saltwater striped bass, bluefish, tarpon, and the like.

the water. It is a good idea also to have several combinations of leaders in various weights and lengths coiled neatly in your tackle box to be available when you want them. These are used mainly for trout, bass, panfish, and for fishing for bait fish in saltwater. The heaviest leaders are for bonefish flies and light bonefish baits, striped bass attractors and rigs used for bluefish, sea trout, snook, tarpon, etc.

FLOATS AND BOBBERS

Several types of floats are used in bait fishing. It is quite easy to select the proper float and rigging combination for your terminal tackle from standard floats available at your tackle store.

Beginning with the lightest of rigs used mainly for fresh water fishing, you have the simple bottle cork that can be attached to the line at the desired depth at which you want the bait to ride in the water. You simply tie the cork on with a square knot and let it go at that. To make the cork moveable along the line for adjustment, drive a nail through it to make a hole and insert the line before attaching the terminal hooks and weights (if any). For the lightest rig use a very small cork or a piece of cork. You can also use bits of foam plastic that come in insulated packages, or you can buy slabs of this foam and cut out just the shape you want for the job at hand. When this is used for bigger fish, it will break off when the fish strikes, leaving the line free of drag so you can enjoy a good battle. Wrap the line around the piece of foam a couple of times and pull it tight. The next pull by the fish will cut right through it and it will fall away. This kind of rig is used by cane pole fishermen and anglers using very basic and simple tackle for all kinds of small fish. Fly fishermen wishing to cast a light bait a long distance use it also. Tarpon fishing in the shallows calls for this type of rig quite often. Sea trout and freshwater trout anglers use this rig to float their live bait into the current.

The Spinning Float

The spinning float is a plastic hollow ball used with equal interest in both fly and light spin fishing. It is a one inch diameter round ball

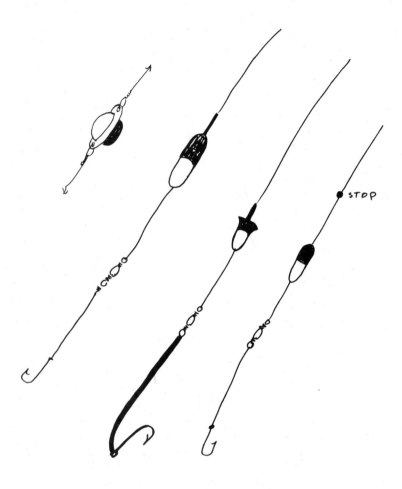

STOP

This is the most common use of the float in a fixed position on the running line. It is tied in and set at a predetermined position in relation to where you want the bait to sink in the water. The leader is attached to the line by a swivel. The float can be slid up and down the line for adjustment, however.

A - Spinning bubble or "bobber."
B - Fixed float.
C - Popping cork float.
D - Sliding cork float rig with a line stop above it to set the depth.

that can be filled or partially filled with water to give it enough weight to cast the terminal tackle properly.

Such floats can be adjusted quickly for depth change and are quite versatile. They are used for bank pole fishing, spinning with lures or bait, and fly fishing with either flies or small baits. The plastic float can also be used in many heavy rigs when it is desired to keep the bait off the bottom, even though the entire rig is heavily weighted to make it possible to make long casts into heavy current or tide. The plastic bubble or bobber can also be attached at the end of the line for easier casting with the bait or baits. Small sinkers are attached as shown.

Fixed Position Floats

The fixed float is very similar in effect and does just what the name implies. It keeps the terminal tackle floating at the desired depth when it is adjusted to the line. These floats come in a number of applicable sizes and a collection of several sizes should be in the tackle box so just the right casting and fishing action is produced. Of the many designs, I suggest the ones with the hollow center and peg. Some have a spring loaded clip, and by merely pressing the button you can attach or remove the float instantly. They are used also at the end of the rig.

Popping Cork Float

The popping cork float is very similar to the others in design and function, but it's designed for surface popping of the float when you twitch and haul back jerkily on your rod tip. This technique is used when it is desired to make the bait look alive. Often the surface disturbance of the popping plug attracts fish to the bait beneath it. These floats are designed somewhat like popping bass plugs, with a hollowed out section at the head that disturbs the water when you pull on it. Some are unweighted, others weighted at the bottom end, so the popping end floats up vertically. When pulled it disturbs the water. When fishing with no sinker near your bait, use the weighted one so the line is directed downward.

Sliding and Casting Float

The sliding and casting float is used mainly when you want the float merely to indicate a strike from the fish, or when it is necessary to keep the bait deep but at an even depth in the current or quiet water. The fixed float would be difficult if not impossible to cast, being so far ahead of the terminal hook, weight, and bait, so the float is designed to slip on the line. The hook is attached to a short leader and then the float is attached to the leader or line above it as shown. A bead or piece of wrap-around wire is wrapped to the line at the desired length. When the cast is made, the float will be at the bottom end where the leader is connected to the line. When the cast is on the water, the float will gradually move up to the stopping point and you are in business. Do not, as some advise, tie a knot in your line and allow the bead to rise to it. It is very difficult to untie a knot. Merely wrap the wrap-around wire (the kind you use on your garbage bags) around a loop in the line, or you can even tie a bow in the line that can be easily untied. A small shirt button can also be used and is quite effective here, when you thread the line through all four holes in the button. This offers enough staying power to offset the pressure from the floating float against it.

Balloon Float

A toy store balloon can be used especially well when you will be fishing your baits a long way from the boat. The balloon is more visible than the smaller floats, lighter in the cast, and will drag far less when you retrieve. Merely inflate the balloon and tie it on the line where you need it: fixed position, or sliding, as you prefer.

The Disappearing Float

Stream trout fisherman, and in fact all freshwater fishing enthusiasts, especially those who use a fly rod or spinning rod, can use a devastating float idea that will carry their bait to the desired position. Anglers working the current lines and tidal estuaries also use this method to their advantage. The float consists of a mere piece of thin wood, any small stick, or even a handy broad leaf.

The line' is merely wrapped around the stick and very lightly inserted into the grain of the wood. The rig is then cast very lightly a very short distance and allowed to float down the current. When the bait arrives at its destination, a sharp pull will dislodge the light float and the bait is then free to drift with the current in a natural way.

Another way to attach it is to fasten a piece of thin paper to the float. At the other end of the paper, the line is wound around in a half bow tie, as shown. The water disintegrates the paper, and the bait is then free to flow with the current. This technique is also used with sinkers. The bait and sinkers go to where they are directed, and when the bait is down there at the correct depth, the sinker falls away allowing the bait to move in the current free from any weight restriction.

HOOKS

Hooks are the business end of the terminal tackle. The all important choice of which hook to use—when, how, and for what fish—can be made once the designs, shapes, weights, strengths, and sizes are known and understood. You'll find that there is a very valid reason for so many hook sizes. Most of the commonly used hooks are available at your tackle store or bait livery along with other items of terminal tackle and bait.

You do not have to select the exact size of hook for specific use. A close approximation is adequate. The small size hooks generally used for freshwater fishing are scaled by a system of straight numbers: for some reason, the larger the number, the smaller the hook. The largest in this class is a #1 and the smallest used for tiny artificial flies and very small baits is a #22.

The saltwater hooks, again for unknown reasons, generally start with the #1/0 and go UP as the hook size enlarges. The largest size of a standard hook is a #20/0.

Hooks are made either from cast steel or steel wire, depending on the designation and use of the hook. The cast hook is strong, but brittle. It can be snapped by too much pressure. Conversely, the wire hook can be bent out straight by too much pressure on it. The following hooks are standard and illustrated with labels for your consideration and choice.

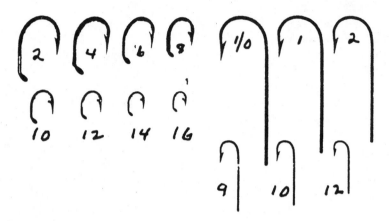

The first batch of hooks shown here are those used for salmon eggs in fishing for steelhead trout and rainbow trout (where salmon eggs are legal bait). Note the short and curved shank and turned down eye. They are also used in tying many of the grub artificial flies and can also be used with actual live grubs, bugs, and worms. They are of wire makeup but have a surprising amount of strength for their size.

The second batch of hooks are long straight-shanked hooks used in the making of snelled hooks, to which leader material is attached. Note they do not have eyes. They're shown as examples of the range of size and hook bend that are available.

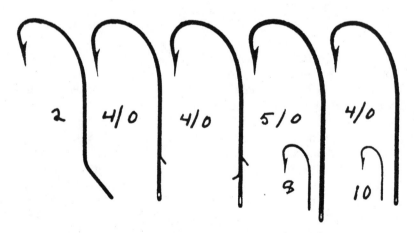

These are called sproat hooks, and you will see here several variations, from the bent shank to the flat eye (not turned up or down, but flat). Some have barbs on the shank to aid the holding of bait. Hooks shown are from size 2 to 10.

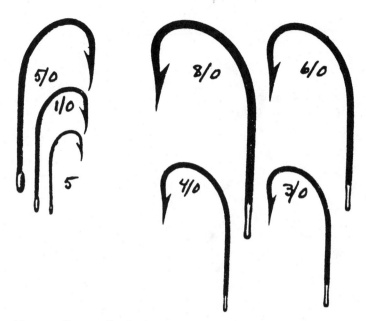

These are flat eye offset hooks used for saltwater fishing. They are also used to tie very heavy freshwater lures and flies, and are used for big fish such as muskellunge, pike, and Pacific salmon. Note the first set have curved barbs and tips. The others have very distinct barb angles and are deadly.

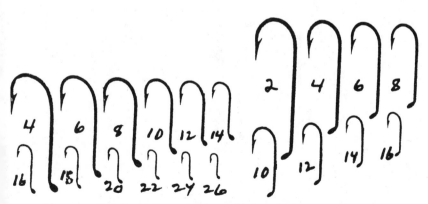

These are primarily freshwater hooks used in bait fishing. Mainly, these turned up eye hooks are used for tying artificial flies, namely Atlantic salmon flies and trolling flies. Sizes range from 2 to 26.

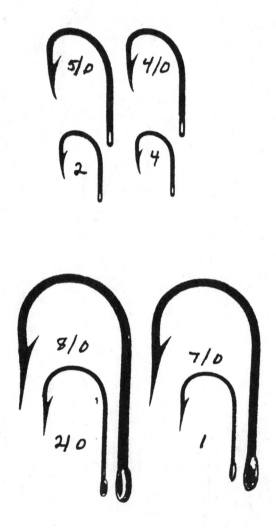

Shown in this batch of hooks is the short shank live bait hook style with the curved point and barb with the flat eye. The Siwash or Pacific salmon hooks from 8/0 to 1 show the range of this style hook.

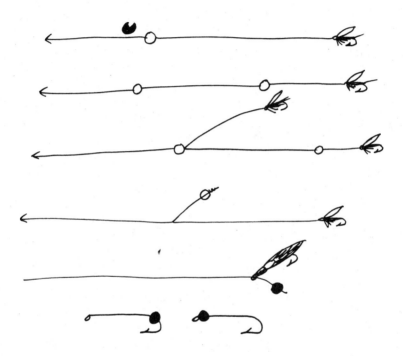

This simple split shot arrangement can take many forms, depending on the tackle, fishing conditions, and fishing objectives. A single split shot of correct size and weight is used for light casting of light lures and baits. When cast with a fly rod, the lightest available is recommended, and two or three spaces a few inches apart will help to make the cast turn properly in the air rather than angle back on itself and cause a tangle.

Rigged as shown is the single shot and two and three shots on the leader. Another way to effectively use the split shot is to tie in a short tippet on the leader and attach the shots to it. Make the leader tippet of much less pound test than the running leader. When the shot gets caught in a snag, you can break it off without losing your terminal hook or lure. Split shot can also be clamped onto the hook as shown.

These are the basic weights used in all kinds of fresh and salt-water fishing with both bait and lure terminal tackle. Each has its specific type of use, though any practical sinker can be used if necessary. They come in various sizes and weights to accommodate almost any need.

1) Beebee shot or split shot sinker. This has a slit cut into it so the weight can be clamped onto the leader or line. They are used singly, or in series, and in combination with other types.

2) The clamp-on sinker, with two ears to be bent over the line to hold it securely from slipping on the line or leader. Several weights and sizes.

3) Wrap-around lead strips. These are used in very light fishing in both fresh and saltwater. The strip is wound tightly around the line or leader at the desired location above the hook, and the end is crimped so that the leader will not slip on the line. Used in conjunction with other weights when necessary. The strip type lead will not tend to snag as quickly as other types of leads and is sometimes easier to cast with light tackle.

4) The slip sinker is merely an oval or round lead with a hole through it, so that the leader can slide free when the sinker is on the bottom. The fish can take the bait almost without any resistance, and when the strike is made, the weight is not affected. Also, the sliding weight is used for heavy casting. The weight stays forward, balancing out the terminal tackle on the cast, and then slips back when the rig settles down on the bottom.

5) The bank sinker is a pear-shaped sinker with a large loop hole on the top. This is used for bottom fishing, and the sinkers are sometimes tied in clusters.

6) The ball sinker, or dipsey sinker, is similar in effect and use as the slip sinker. Instead of the sinker with the hole through it, the sinker is attached to the line by a small ring at its top.

7) The diamond sinker is used in bottom, surf, and bay fishing under muddy and sandy conditions. The point is supposed to sink into the mud and find its way into the small gravel to hold the rig on the bottom.

8) The pyramid sinker is the favorite of surf fishermen and those who fish sandy bottoms. This sinker grabs the bottom and holds on.

9) The trolling sinker is attached to the line through its two rings. By doubling the loop of the line, the sinker can be moved back

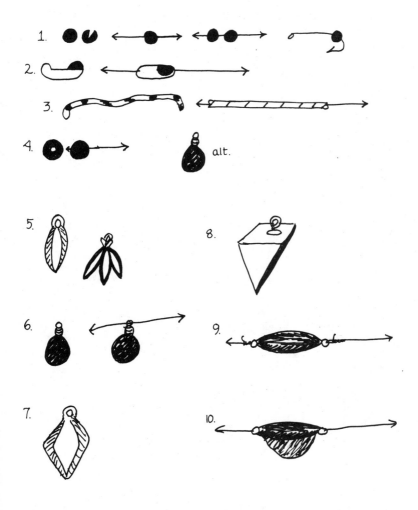

1.

2.

3.

4.   alt.

5.   8.

6.   9.

7.   10.

and forth to the desired position on the line in relation to the lure or hook.

10) The trolling fin sinker is the same functioning sinker but has a finlike shape to attempt to keep the line from twisting.

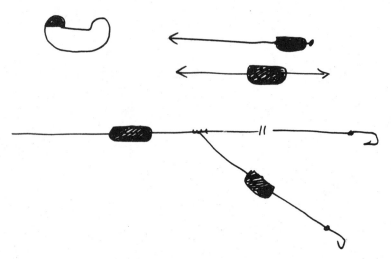

The simple clamp-on sinker comes in several light weights for various uses and is used in the same way as the split shot and for the same purposes. It can be removed much easier than the split shot, however, and is sometimes much easier to slide along the leader without roughing the leader material. Like the split shot, it can be attached to a fine leader tippet for easy breakoff or to take off if conditions require.

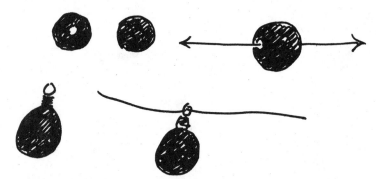

The sliding egg sinker can be attached directly to the leader if it is to be a long one. The bait will ride free when a fish takes it, or it can be attached to the actual running line ahead of the leader connection. The object in using it is for the bait to run free once the fish has taken the bait in its mouth. Pressure from a static bait might cause the fish to drop the bait. On cast, the weight will push forward on the line or leader but will slip back when the rig hits the bottom. The dipsey sinker, tied in as shown, will perform the same function and is preferred by many.

In order for additional weight to be used when necessary, a split shot can be added to the line ahead and behind the range of the slip sinker to keep it in bounds, as shown.

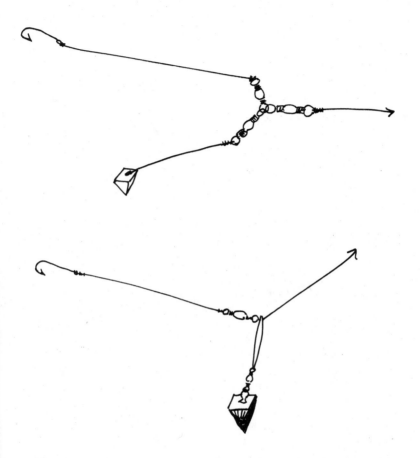

The pyramid sinker is the surf fisherman's standby, for it will hold to the sandy bottom better than the egg sinker or any of the others. It is made in several weights and sizes that will accommodate light to very heavy surf rods and terminal rigs, depending on the species of fish sought. There are several ways of attaching the weight in relation to other items of the surf terminal tackle. The most common is with the use of the three-way swivel as shown. When fishing in areas where crabs and bottom snags are numerous, a small bottle cork is also tied into the bait leader to raise it off the bottom.

A second rig for this weight and one or two hook terminal is to attach it before the swivel on a wire loop that can be made or purchased for such use. When the cast is made, the weight will be pressured toward the swivel, but when the cast drifts down to the bottom, the line and hook are free in the same way they would be if a slip sinker were being used.

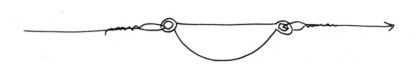

The trolling sinker has not been improved upon for a hundred years or more and is tied in as shown on a wire leader. It is better to attach it to the line, with swivels fore and aft to keep it from twisting the line. Some of these sinkers are kidney shaped and others are slim like a bean. Some even have a planning head, so attach the head toward the basic line rather than the terminal tackle for best use. They also are made in various weights to accommodate both casting and deep or shallow trolling, depending on the speed of the boat and size and strength of the rod and reel.

A sacrifice rig for your sinker is easy to tie in. This is used when it is desired to have the weight break away so that the bait, once on or near the bottom, will flow free. Using thread or very fine monofilament, wrap the ends extending from the lead weight around the leader and its connection to the line, but make sure that it is brought up tight enough to slacken the length of material on the main line. When the fish strikes, the line will straighten out and thereby pull the loosely wound lead lines loose and the weight will drop away.

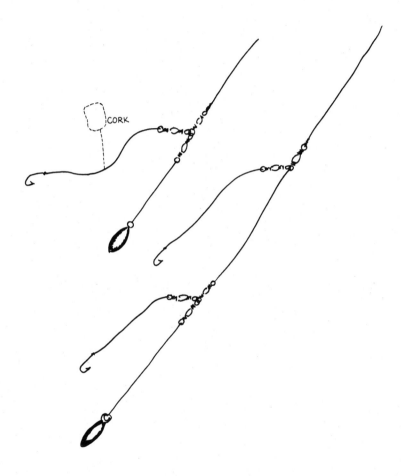

Shown here is the conventional and very versatile bottom fishing rig that is used in both fresh and saltwater fishing. It is used with various weight lines and leaders, hooks, and sinkers. The one or two tandem leaders can be tied into the main line by the use of the blood knot with a leader extension, or they can be attached with the use of three-way swivels as shown. The weight is attached to the very end of the leader for better casting efficiency.

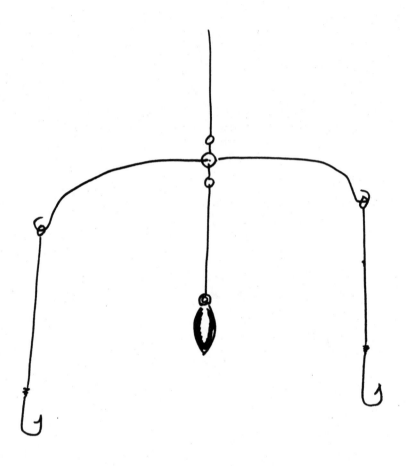

While the familiar spreader rig is used primarily in saltwater fishing, it has found its use in some freshwater angling also. The actual rig itself can be purchased at the tackle store and attached to the line as shown, with the weight set in the middle. Not an easy rig to cast, the spreader is merely dropped overboard with its baited hooks to await action.

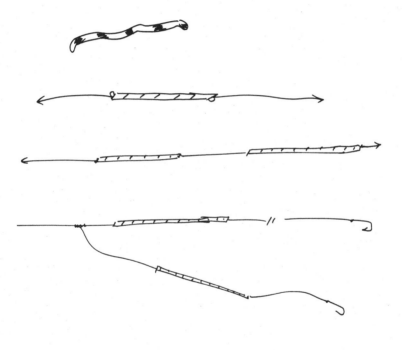

The wrap-around lead sinker is most versatile for both fresh and light saltwater angling when conventional and bulky weights are found wanting. By merely wrapping the lead strip around the leader at the desired location, the very light weight will often be just what is needed to make the lure or bait act the way you want and also to travel at the desired depth. Shown here are several rigs and uses for the wrap-around lead.

Baits

FRESHWATER BAITS

Baits for freshwater fishing are numerous and deadly, when hooked on properly and presented in a natural way to the fish. There are many kinds of natural baits usually found right in or near the very water you will be fishing in. They can be netted, hook-caught, or purchased live in containers at the local bait livery or tackle store. Most resorts have tackle counters and bait sources available. The independent fisherman, however, can go equipped with tackle to catch his own bait, and so be able to fish even when the bait store is closed.

You can usually entice minnows and other so-called rough fish by throwing bread crumbs into the water near the shore and enticing the minnows in close enough to net them. Use either a fine mesh mounted on your long handled landing net or a cast net or minnow trap that can either be bought or constructed from simple materials. Crawfish can be gathered at night along stream edges and lake shores with the use of a flash light and a dip net, or again, they can be trapped much as lobsters are trapped in the ocean: with a specially constructed trap. Worms, night crawlers, and grubs can be taken from dung piles or dug out from damp turf. Night crawlers can be gathered by night with a flash light. They are best found on golf courses with their very rich earth and usually will be seen above ground. Grab at them and you fill your jar in no time.

Keeping bait alive and healthy requires veritable aquariums with adequate water circulation, enough fresh water, and sufficient space. While this is quite a project for the average angler, it is the best way to go. If you live by or near the water, you can also close off a small section of shoreline and mesh it in to contain your bait fish. It's easiest to purchase your bait fish from a bait dealer. To maintain the fish, you keep them in large containers with adequate aeration. There are two kinds of bait cans built for this purpose. One is for the main supply and the other is for on-the-spot fishing. A bait can is designed to sink in the water where you will be fishing on shore. Tied to a rope, it will stay with you, and you can move it when you want to try another location. This same ventilated pail is also used aboard the boat. It is carried inside when underway and cast overboard on a rope when you are still fishing. Bait basins are also built into many fishing boats: water flows in and out constantly to keep the fish healthy and breathing.

Baits for ice fishing usually are minnows, perch, and sunfish worked on the bottom. Live or cut bait can also be used.

Freshwater baits need not always be alive. Dead minnows are often used, and cut bait—pieces of minnow—are very effective for many game and food fish. You can buy preserved minnows in small jars at any tackle store.

Frogs, toads, salamanders, grass shrimp, crickets, grasshopper grubs, and the like can be used as bait when dead. Worms, however, are best used alive when possible.

The following are the best and most popular baits used in freshwater fishing and also those that are readily available at bait stores and liveries.

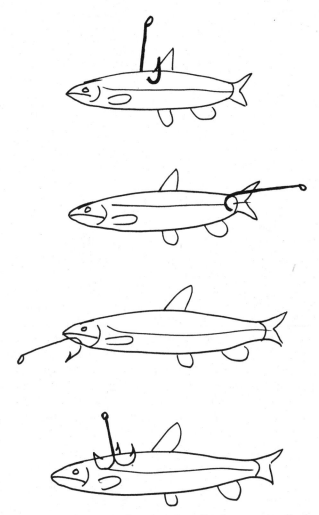

Live minnows account for more large catches of big bass, trout, and other game fish and include also the smaller panfish such as crappie, bluegill, and the like. There are many ways to hook minnows.

1) Hook through the back for still fishing and drift fishing.

2) Hook through the tail for bottom fishing.

3) Hook through the underlip for casting and trolling. Fished dead, for trolling and casting, hook through the entire head.

4) Double hook rigs can also be used effectively.

Small live sunfish, bream, and the like are best hooked through the lower lip if you wish to fish them alive for a long period.

The "angle" worm, otherwise called earthworm or wiggler, is probably the most universal bait used to catch both fresh and saltwater fish. The best kind for trout, bass and panfish are the little red worms found in dung piles. Ordinary earth worms taken from the garden or from grassy earth are also good when allowed to flush out and become hard and firm. Shown here are the many ways to attach the earth worm to the hook for specific fishing purposes. When possible, run the hook through the "collar" or egg sac of the worm, for this is the toughest part of the insect. Shown here also is the proper way to rig the worm on a spinner or spoon hook.

Night crawlers, the larger variety of worm, are equally good for catching small fish, if only a small piece is used on a small hook. Generally the bigger fish will take the whole night crawler with relish.

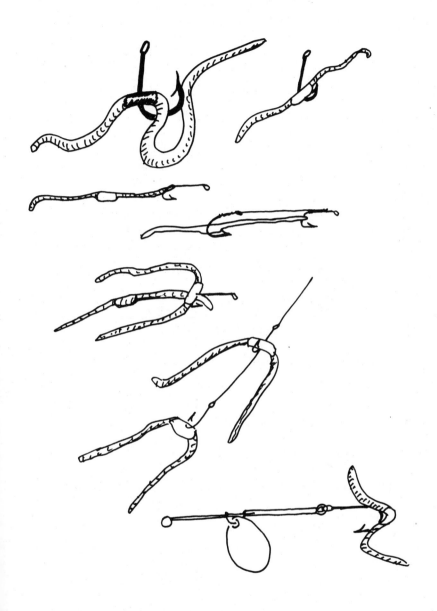

Crickets and grasshoppers are among the most popular baits for panfish, trout, and bass and can easily be obtained in the fields and woodlands adjacent to the fishing area. Grasshoppers are usually logy and inactive at dawn when the dew is on the ground, and they can be caught easily by hand. Keep them in a glass jar with holes punched in the top for air. They will stay alive for at least twenty-four hours. Hook through the collar if the hook is small, or directly through the body if a larger hook is used. If you wish to fish them alive, try attaching them with a very small rubber band cut from a small rubber hose. Crickets are also easily obtainable, though not as common in the fields as hoppers. Hook them in the same way.

Crawfish, or crayfish, as they are sometimes called, are found along the edges of streams, ponds, and even lakes shores. They should be caught at night when they are readily seen feeding in the shallows. You have to be quick with your small dip net. Keep them in a well aereated bait pail and change the water often. Remove the claws or they will tend to destroy each other. Fish take them better when they do not have claws. Hook through the ridge just behind the head to keep them alive or you can hook them in the last section of the body in front of the tail. Fish them with or without weights.

Live frogs are possibly the best bait for bass, walleyed pike, pickerel, and even pike and musky. Common varieties found near the fishing area are best, since the fish know about them and seek them out in the shallows and pad flats. They are easy to keep alive without water. Just keep in a cool container.

They should be hooked by one leg if you want to keep them alive for a long time. The underlip hook is better than hooking through both lips, since they will be able to breathe easier. Some anglers hook them through the backbone, but they soon die from this, and hooking them through the back skin will not assure their staying on the hook for long.

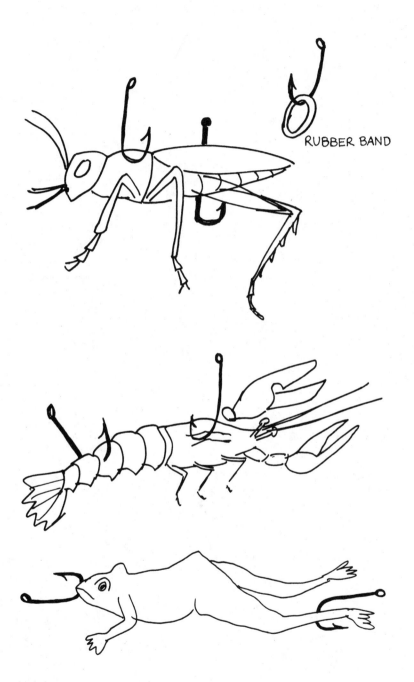

RUBBER BAND

Caterpillars and grubs are also very good baits when fished dead drift in the current or still fished. Hook them entirely through their body since they are very soft and can come off the hook readily when cast or pulled through the current. They are actually as good a bait as the earthworm, though not always readily available. Grubs, bonnet worms, and sand maggots are also good substitutes.

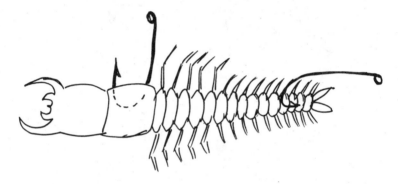

The helgramite is possibly the most popular bass bait that you can take from the water. It is the larvae of the dobson fly. Tough to find and catch, they can be found by overturning logs and rocks along the stream or lake shore. But be not surprised if you get nipped. Hook the helgramite through the collar near the head of the insect to keep it alive as long as possible. The larger ones can be hooked near the tail or even all the way through the body as shown. Fished dead drift, on the bottom, or cast and slowly retrieved are the ways to work this bait.

Small grass shrimp are found in many freshwaters and most bait stores, particularly in the South. Stores carry them either dead or in preserve bottles. Unless they are large, use two or three on the hook, and hook them through the top of the back ridge if using very small hooks, or entirely through the body with standard hooks. When fishing for bait to fish for bigger fish, use just the back end of the body on a size 16 or smaller hook.

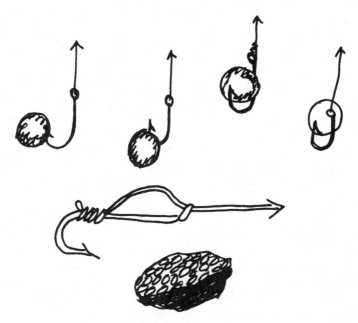

Salmon eggs, where legal, are deadly on trout, particularly rainbow and cut-throat trout. They are also used for steelhead when they are migrating upstream. More often, however, steelhead rigs call for steelhead egg clusters, also shown here.

A) How to hook a single salmon egg.

B) Hooking the steelhead eggs cluster.

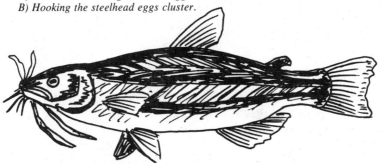

Catfish baits can be made up of almost anything from worms to chicken wings, animal guts, and dubious mixtures of rotten flesh mixed with dough or even cotton balls. They also like caterpillars. Quite often, they will take baits being used to catch other fish, especially when the bait is found in quiet water and under muddy conditions. Beef or pork liver is another goodie that cats like, and, of course, if you have some left over frozen shrimp or any frozen fish that can be tightly impaled on a hook, use it. Catfish like their baits on the bottom, and they usually take a good amount of time sniffing at it, mouthing it, and then finally taking it deep into their mouths.

SALTWATER BAITS

There are literally hundreds of saltwater bait fish that can be used in saltwater fishing. They are available wherever the game fish are located, since the bigger fish feed on them naturally. Quite often it is possible to either net or hook-catch bait fish right where you are fishing for the big species. Surf fishermen catch mullet, for example, with cast nets, while they are watching their rods that are stationed in rod holders with the line cast out.

The basic idea is to feed the game fish what they feed on most of the time. These bait fish, either alive, dead, frozen, whole, or cut, are available at docks, fishing piers, tackle stores and marinas, or you can catch your own. How to keep them alive depends on the species and type. Crabs, for example, can stay out of water for quite a while, but minnows and bait fish must be maintained in their natural element.

Party boats, charter cruisers, and even the smallest of saltwater fishing boats generally have live bait wells built into the hull design for the specific purpose of keeping the bait alive and well. Bait cans used in freshwater angling can also be used.

Cut and frozen bait must be kept in a container that is insulated, so the flesh does not become too soft to attach to the hook or get mushy, and thus not attractive to the fish. The following are basic saltwater baits and the ways to hook them for specific game fish being sought.

RIGGED BAITS FOR BIG GAME FISHING

Specially rigged baits, dead whole fish that are skillfully wrapped and hooked so that they ride naturally in the water, are a must for successful big game fishing. The object is to imitate, with a dead fish, the free running live fish that the big fish will follow and take while it is being trolled or cast. Some of these baits are small, minnow size and others can range up to a 4- or 5-pound bonefish when marlin are being sought.

It has taken some mighty inventive saltwater guides many years to devise methods of leader making and dressing of the bait fish to the leader and hooks in order to approximate the real live attractors as previously shown.

BAIT AND LURE COMBINATIONS

While a great amount of bait fishing, with both live and dead bait, is done without added attractors such as spoons, plugs, spinners, and series of spinners, these attractors certainly do make a difference under certain conditions.

The fiddler crab is one of the most traditional baits for use from the northern to the southern states for sheepshead, snapper, redfish, grouper, drum, and even for striped bass, snook, and at times, sea trout and porgies. You can buy them or find them near where you will do your fishing. They can scamper quickly to their holes and it is fun chasing them about. Contain them in a can with some seaweed and a little water. They do not have dangerous claws. In fact, their claws are quite weak, but will give you a startling pinch. They are best fished with the claws removed. If they reach the bottom they can hold onto almost anything, and so become unavailable to the fish you are after.

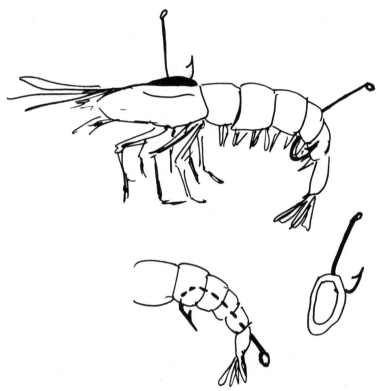

The most versatile, popular, and successful salt water fishing bait is the shrimp—preferably live. Dead shrimp and cut pieces of shrimp are also used in some cases quite successfully, especially for the smaller species.

Live shrimp are generally available at the bait shops, tackle shops, and marinas. You can buy them live and keep them in a bucket designed for the purpose. They must have fresh, clean water constantly, however, to keep them in an active state.

The best way to hook a live shrimp is through the straight edge found on the head of the shrimp. Do not go too deep with the hook however, or you will kill the shrimp. That tough ridge is quite enough to attach a hook to, even a trebble. When casting, try to merely swing the bait, and avoid snapping it out. Hooking it in this way allows it to move about freely. When fishing in shallow water, make sure your bobber will keep it well off the bottom away from the crabs.

Threading the shrimp is another way to hook it and is far more durable than hooking it in the head ridge, although it does tend to drown the shrimp. Threading is best done with dead shrimp, and to keep them moving actively like a live one, use rod action and keep the bait moving and jiggling in the water. Thread the bait as shown.

Still another way to use the shrimp involves the use of a small rubber band which is placed around the shrimp as shown and the hook slipped into the space between the band and the shrimp.

Sand fleas are a bait that is quite popular with saltwater anglers whenever they are found. Pompano love them, as do other saltwater species found along the surfline. Available at boat liveries, baitstores, and tackle stores, you can also pick them up along the beach on a receding wave as you see them digging into the sand. Place them in a can of water and keep giving them fresh water to keep them alive. Hook as shown. They make an ideal bait for ultralight spinning and fly rod fishing in the surf, or they can be used as an alternate bait with shrimp, mullet, or other northern bait fish.

Legal size crawfish make as ideal a bait as shrimp and, when possible, use them for snapper, grouper and under the right conditions, even for tarpon and snook. This is mainly a southern bait, found in Florida and the coastline of the southern states. There are two basic ways to hook the crawfish, somewhat similar to hooking shrimp. The first is for casting with the hook inserted as shown (A). The body hooking (B) is better used for still fishing.

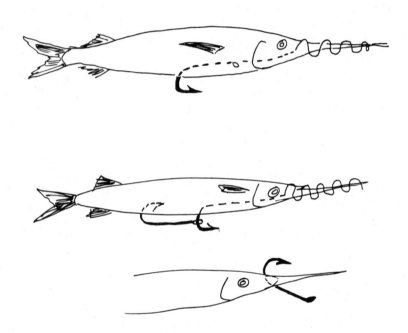

While the ballyhoo is primarily a southern bait used for sailfish, there are equally good substitutes in the northern waters when the bait fish is rigged as shown. They are fished live, cast, or trolled, just so long as they are kept on or near the surface. Insert the hook into the mouth as shown, point upward, and allow it to come out through the upper jaw.

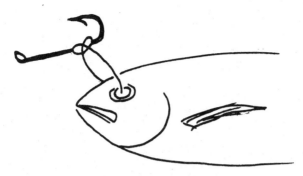

Rigging the live bonito or other equally available saltwater food/game fish can be done as shown. While difficult to come by except by angling for them, they do make a very good bait for big game fish, as do mackerel and other species. Most good guides fish for them while the angler is trolling for the bigger game. Once hooked, the bait is quickly rigged while still alive and then put overboard to search out the big fish such as tuna, sailfish, marlin, and the like. If you are in a particular hurry, merely hook the bonito through the lower lip. Wiring it through the eyes and onto the hook is the next best rig.

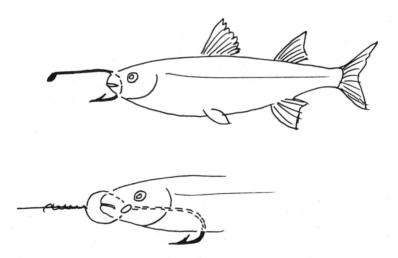

Mullet, anchovy, herring, tinker mackerel, and pilchard can all be rigged as shown for casting and trolling. This variety of ways can also be added to, depending on the conditions and tackle to be used. The first way is to hook the bait through the mouth, and for a more secure holding, through the eye. Hooking this way is for trolling where bait spin is held to a minimum. The bait fish can also be hooked in the back near the dorsal fin for still and drift fishing. For bottom fishing, the hook should be inserted near the tail, leaving the fish free to travel downward to the bottom.

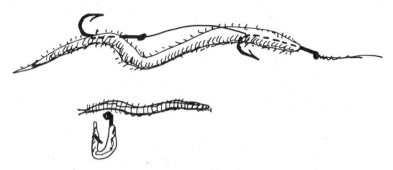

All marine worms have soft bodies. Worms such as sandworms, blood worms, and clam worms are very good to entice striped bass, bluefish, tuna, and a host of southern fish such as tarpon, snook, and bottom fish such as red snapper. You can rig the whole worm as shown, or bits and pieces, depending on what you are after. Small bits can be used to catch bait fish to be used on the game species. Rig as shown.

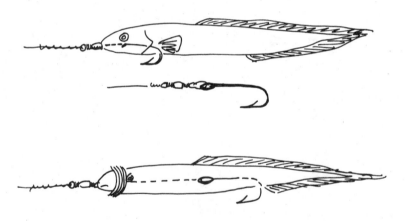

Eel for trolling and heavy casting have been a favorite of striped bass fishermen for a century. The whole eel can be used as shown, or just the eel skin for a lighter, easier-to-cast combination. Skins are attached to the lead head as shown and generally rigged with two hooks some inches apart on brass chain leaders. The back eye of the swivel is sewn into the mouth, and the thread is wrapped tightly around the head.

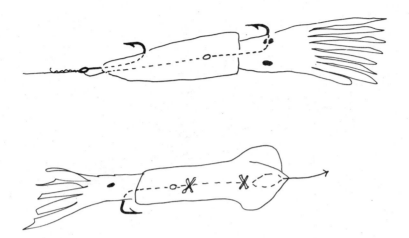

Drifting squid rigs are legion and have been developed over the years by innovative guides and anglers. The most popular rig is shown and it's quite simple. A two hook rig is made with the hooks inserted as in the diagram. This makes a very good bait for drift fishing.

When it is necessary to rig the squid for trolling or drifting, rig as shown below. Tie in a small egg sinker right against the squid tail with the hook in the position almost to the head. Insert the baiting needle into the strong part of the head and pull the leader inside the mantle until the sinker takes up the position indicated. Then sew the mantle to the leader and tighten the connection of head to mantle with x-shape stitches.

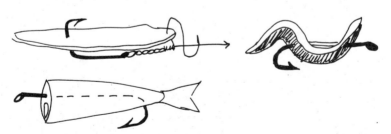

Shown here are various ways of rigging strip baits, pieces of fish that have been cleanly cut, either as fillets, or headless for easier hooking. These can also be hook-rigged behind a jig or other lure for casting and trolling.

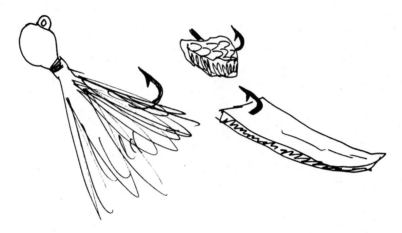

    Jigging has become a most popular way to catch many saltwater species, from northern pollock and striped bass to the myriad of fish to be taken as far south as the Florida Keys. Shown here are several suggestions for rigging and attaching bits of bait to the jig.

Fishing Necessities and Accessories

You can fill a station wagon with a lot of gear that is not really necessary. Of course, the amount of gear you use depends on your personality and the amount of time, space, and patience you have. Quite often it is possible to go with a minimum of equipment, aside from your actual tackle and gear, but more often than not, when conditions allow, it is better to have extra gear than be found wanting.

The following pages show all types of fishing gear and accessories that would amount to a bare minimum for your full enjoyment. There are always alternatives and new products coming on the market. As I always warn, be careful of so-called bargains in this department. Buy only good equipment, care for it, and it will last you a lifetime. Broken equipment or quick wear-out is no bargain and can seriously restrict your fishing sport if it goes sour when you need it most.

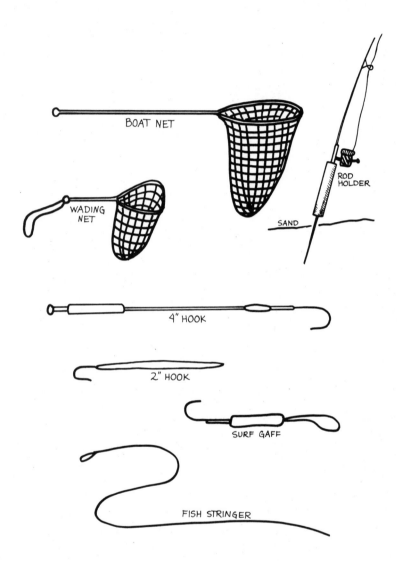

PART TWO

Freshwater Bait Fishing

TECHNIQUES FOR CATCHING PANFISH

Much of the technique involved in bait fishing is quite similar to that employed when fishing artificial lures and flies, though more care must be exercised to avoid jarring natural bait off the hook. Essentially, bait fishing limits the casting distance, demanding the angler be closer to his target area in order to reach the fish. He has, however, the added enticement of appeal, namely natural foods on which fish feed and a few man-made concoctions to boot!

Panfish are the "little fish," not including any carp that may be encountered in impoundments and reservoirs. And, little fish are the most plentiful and widely distributed. They're readily available so, unless one lives in the Gobi Desert, good fishing can probably be found not too far from one's own back porch.

Terminal tackle is as important here as in the case of fishing diverse waters for other species. Lightweight spinning gear, the fly rod and light bait casting combinations can be used. While the pan-fisherman will possibly do some casting and trolling, angling for panfish is best done by still fishing (involving very short casts), and "dunking," that is, walking along the shoreline of a lake or river and tossing the bait out as far as possible. Baits include worms, grasshoppers, frogs, minnows and nonindigenous baits such as pork rind.

Bait Lake Stillfishing

The technique is relatively simple. The lake to be fished may contain sunfish, crappie, bluegill and maybe small bass. There may also be a smattering of white and yellow perch, which is an excellent group to go after. Armed with the terminal rigs, the modern light fly rod or light spinning rod is selected. Locate a portion of the lake either out of the direct wind or where the breeze is blowing away from the shore. Look for indentations in the shoreline where large rocks and boulders, possible grass and lilypad beds, provide ample cover and natural food. Select a location out from the brush and trees to permit free use of the tackle, but not cluttered with water grasses and snags. Cast an unweighted worm, hopper or hooked minnow as far out from shore as possible. Sinkers may not be needed at all. If the current is not too fast nor the water too deep, try to keep the bait as deep as possible without snagging the bottom. The plastic bubble or even a mere bottle cork may be all that is necessary to keep the bait from snagging. If fishing on a lazy-current river, select a quiet deadwater stretch where the bank is high or where rushes form deep holes or pockets.

Catfish and even carp can be rendered on the following baits: For catfish, especially in rivers where the big ones abound, use tasties such as Limburg cheese. Mix it with dough for more holding power on the hook, or use a small plastic bag of see-through thickness and fill it with bait and set it to the hook. Sour meat, clams, rotting fish bait or innards from fish previously caught will work equally well. If expecting to fish a specific location regularly, try and find dead birds or old meat of any kind; place them in a sack that's weighted down with gravel or stones. Catfish, carp, etc. will flock to it.

Drifting, Casting, Trolling

The fisherman who owns a small rowboat or canoe, or who can rent one at the lake of his choice should begin by surveying the waters in an excursion cruise. Of course, if the lake or waterway is extensive, such a cruise would depend heavily on individual circumstances and preference. When possible, note where other fishermen are working, and look for stream outlets, deep cut-ins, sheltered coves, sharp points of land, weed-choked bays and rocky shores where the water is reasonably deep. All of these conditions can lead fish to live bait offerings without the need for trolling deep spots or spring holes. When the fishing area has been selected, (and assuming favorable wind direction) rig with minnows or worms, two hooks and a light sinker. Plan to cast this rigging overboard and merely drift along in the breeze. If the course is near shore, drop a line and sinker down once in a while to check the depth. If the lake is fairly shallow, use a bobber adjusted to the correct depth. Upon approaching the shore, a reef or mid-lake grass flat, try anchoring and cast the baits. If the water is deep, say over the ten-foot mark, try trolling slowly, using slightly heavier weights.

Ice Fishing

There's no need to store away fishing gear when the lake freezes over, because then fishing isn't limited to pan or coarse fish. One may catch pike, musky, bass and even trout. Fishing regulations during this period, however, are usually prohibitive and declare "closed season" on most game fish. But fish species illegal by this method in one area may be legal in another. The fiserman should know these laws; neglect them and he'll probably catch cold and a chillier fine!

Tip-ups are generally used for ice fishing. These are simple contraptions baited on lines equipped with a signalling device. This device is designed to alert the angler that a fish is tugging the bait.

It is a cold sport and dreary winter winds will bite reddened noses and chill dispositions. But ice fishing is great fun, especially in the company of fellow anglers with whom to share hot coffee, fishing yarns and tackle techniques. It can be time well spent.

To merely try some fishing luck with a hand line, simply cut a hole in the ice with an axe, drop the baited line into the hole, stand there and wait. The conventional ice fishing rig is, however, preferred; therefore make several tip-ups and set up a windbreak. Bring along a camp stove, comfortable camp chair and be prepared to sit beneath the winter sky and watch the tip-ups for action.

When the flag goes up this does not necessarily mean the fish is hooked. It may be merely "fooling around" with the bait. Quite often, if action stops, it's wise to bring the line in and inspect the bait. Part of the ice fishing technique is to know precisely when to haul back the line to set the hook. Endeavor to wait until the fish starts a full run-off before snubbing him.

Introducing Others to Fishing Pleasure

The experience gained by fishing for the somewhat less glamorous panfish is always profitable in fishing for the more active varieties. It helps, for instance, in mastering the choice of tackle and terminal gear, the art of simple short distance casting and the tricks of hooking fish that stubbornly "fool" with the bait. It helps in learning where and how to get the best bait, whether from the field or storebought. It would be a shame to bungle a potentially thrilling experience with a big bass, trout, pike, musky and even catfish by going unprepared—tacklewise—without regard to the various fishing conditions and gear limitations that are often encountered when the action gets hot.

Over the years, there should be plenty of chance to fish for the "proud ones," but it may come as a surprise to find easy fishing for the smaller species (especially if close to home) a delightful recourse offering many hours of outdoor relaxation.

Where there are youngsters around or neighborhood kids, invite them along—instruct as necessary, and offer them a taste of the good life they might otherwise miss.

For recreation, general education and profitable tips on fishing and outdoor life, it pays to join a rod and gun club. The exchange of information and feeling of brotherhood in such groups is quite intense. These organizations make sure conservation and antipollution efforts are pushed through to the lawmakers. Also, it pays to make a good friend of the game warden, or forest ranger; these fellows can often be very helpful.

TECHNIQUES FOR GAME FISH

Now the bait fisherman enters the realm of the "big time"; he's after prize brook, brown, rainbow, steelhead, dolly varden and lake trout; large and smallmouth bass, pickerel, pike, muskellunge and large catfish. That's quite an order, but he's all set, having "rehearsed" much of the technique and tackle selection with smaller fish. He now knows something about where to look for good fishing spots in lakes and rivers. He's familiar with casting, and makes an intelligent choice whether to try drifting, trolling or casting over some specific location with the appropriate tackle. Handling bait has become almost second nature. He's snagged the bottom several times, gotten tangled, lost a few fish by strikes that happened too soon, too hard and too fast. He's lost some from allowing too much slack in the line. In short, he's learned both the agony and ecstasy of bait fishing.

Collecting bait or buying it from local bait and tackle dealers is now a set proposition. When in his boat, he now remembers to place his tackle box out of the way and to stack his rods so they won't get tangled or stepped on. In toto, the routine of fishing is now a part of him and no longer the strange, new project he may once have only dreamt about.

It is time to go after the gamesters and, searching throughout the area in which he lives, he knows what species are available. If he is planning a trip or vacation, he'll head for lakes and rivers that abound with the preferred species.

In fishing for the game species, the accent must be on action. The fisherman will be hooking fish that may grab his bait with ferocious energy and take off before he will have had time to react or prepare. Or, the fish may lazily mouth the bait, necessitating the patience to hold back before setting the hook. Playing these fish requires working knowledge gained from experience in tackle use. One learns just how far to strain the rod, especially with those lively ones that can either run all the line out in fast water or take terminal gear to the bottom and snag it in order to escape the meancing hook.

The terrific power of a one-pound rainbow trout or a four-pound largemouth bass is amazing. And a ten-pound pike will give turbulent battle. With luck (one of the few times it's needed) you may even land a twenty-five pound musky!

There will also be days when no matter how well the fisherman handles his tackle he'll probably return home fishless. Somehow even fish have their "day of rest," and simply refuse to nibble. Fishing, like other sports, has its delightful frustrations.

Large or Smallmouth Bass

Large and smallmouth bass are primarily lake fish though the smallmouth is often found in fast streams. Depending on the conditions, fishing methods are: casting, trolling, still and drift fishing. When the lakes are high in the spring, cast to or troll by the shorelines directly into the grass and overhangs. As the season progresses and where legal, bass can be taken in their spawning grounds by casting and/or trolling. Later, they will be found during the early morning

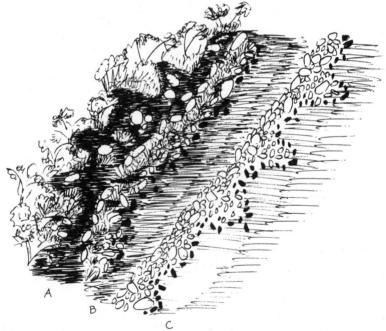

A. Spring high water
B. Midseason normal
C. Late season low water

Variance of shore line during fall season

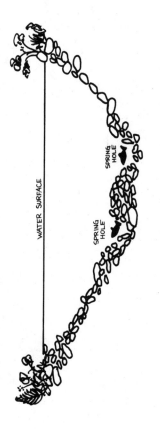

WATER SURFACE

SPRING HOLE

SPRING HOLE

Diagram of typical lake cross-section

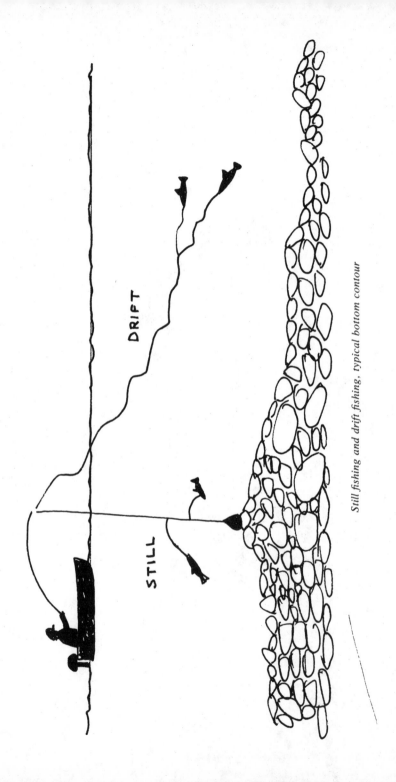

Still fishing and drift fishing, typical bottom contour

hours and at night along the shore, or deep in the cold-temperature belts and spring holes by still or drift fishing. Earthworms, night-crawlers and live bait such as yellow perch (a fish with more stamina than the minnow) or frogs are strongly recommended. Crawfish are excellent, cast unweighted at dusk or nightime along the grassy shore where there are holes among the rocks.

Seek protected bays and coves for casting and sharp points of land for trolling and still fishing. When fishing an unfamiliar lake, inquire about the hot spots at the local tackle store and chew the fat with fellow anglers at the boat dock. Observe where other anglers fish and how they are doing it, particularly those who come into the dock with loaded fish stringers!

When night fishing from the shore, make sure to walk the shore-line the day before. *Do not venture into a strange territory after dark.* When fishing from a boat at night keep light to a minimum, because even a dim flash scares bass and blinds the fisherman for minutes afterward. Learn to tie knots and select prearranged ter-minal tackle and bait without having to use a light: fishermen who can do this will be much better off. Remember not to go out alone: always take a friend when fishing at night. This is generally the best time to fish the big ones during the hot summer since they seem to bite oftener at night.

Trout

Trout fishing in lakes is a tricky proposition. During the early season just after the ice is out, trout surface for a few weeks, feeding on small flies and minnows. Take them with unweighted baits such as worms, nymphs, impaled insects and live minnows, by casting, near-surface trolling or drift fishing. Mornings or evenings when the wind is down are the best times and groups of trout can be found where they feed.

Trout of the big rivers will be found in the slackwaters, below bends and in big, deep pools. Since there is some current action, dead minnows can be used though live ones are frequently better.

As the season progresses, lake trout will seek the cool waters of stream outlets or spring holes. Locate these areas and troll across them, dropping the baits to various depths. During the summer, river

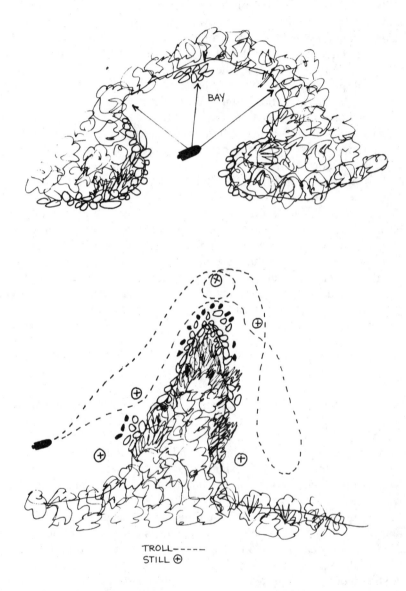

BAY

TROLL-----
STILL ⊕

Suggested pattern of fishing cove and point

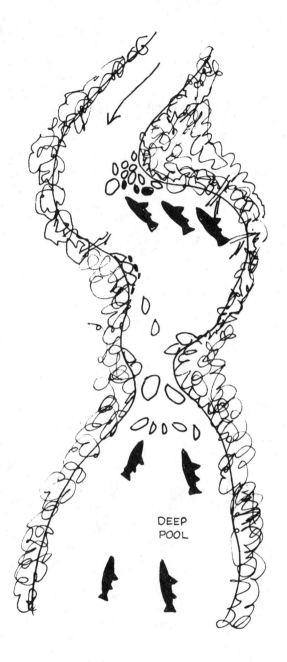

Where the fish lie in the current

trout will similarly seek out aerated water, so fish for them directly below the breaks in rapids and in fast-water slicks.

Light to medium gear is required, though heavy weights may not be needed as terminal tackle unless one plans to work the deepest portions of the lake. Here again, find out as much as can be learned from the "locals" and consult geodetic maps for lake contours. Use a thermometer, seek depths where temperatures range from sixty to seventy degrees. Knowing the proper depth is most important in lake fishing, especially during the summer season. Night, or at least

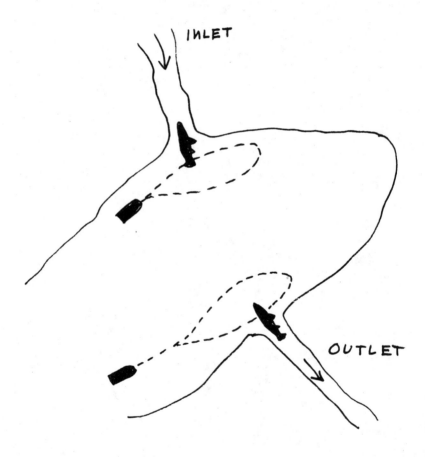

Ways to cover inlets and outlets

predawn fishing is preferred if there is heavy boating activity during the day.

All manner of aquatic insects can be used; don't neglect the grasshopper.

Lake Trout and Walleye Pike

Quite often these two species are found in the same lake. They're both bait fishing exclusives though they can be enticed with artificial lures, too. Best combination for casting and medium trolling is a spoon or set of spinners followed by cut fish bait or rigged dead minnow. Only in the spring will these two be taken near the surface and usually near stream outlets. Fish for them in deep water by very slow trolling, using wire lines and heavy sinkers for bait; or sinkers, spoons, spinners and bait. The medium weight bait casting rod, or specialized trolling rod is an excellent choice, either with level–wind bait casting reel or large capacity spinning reel.

Since these fish are found in big lakes, there is a great deal of territory to explore. One may spend an entire season in blind fishing and never hit the hot spots. But as suggested in previous pages, cull information from every available source. The conservation offices of the various states have excellent publications and distribute current fishing reports for the particular state, including stocking dates and general conditions. Write to them. Resort owners must keep informed and up-to-date with regard to such information for the benefit of their patrons. So don't be afraid to ask about the hot spots; bone up also on rigs and tackle combinations that are paying off locally.

Lake fishing can be a boring and unrewarding proposition when fishing over barren waters. So the most important part of this fishing will be to inquire first and fish later. A good source of information are places selling bait. Also when possible watch the anglers in nearby boats and (without being too obvious) try to fish near where they're hauling 'em in.

Pike and Musky

Now, combine what's been related about trout, bass, lake trout and walleye. Then to be all set, go equipped with much heavier gear.

These two fish, the biggest and fiercest, are found in lakes, fast and slow rivers and interlinked streams. Their homeland, generally in northern country, abounds with brush-cluttered streams and shore-lines littered with driftwood, snags and big bouldered coves and bays. The best seasons are spring and fall.

These are big fish and require a hardy morsel to attract them. While artificial lures take big ones once in a while, the bait fisherman really has the edge if he goes with adequate tackle to handle the presentation of the bait and the power of the fish. Small catfish and lake chubs are the best baits. The deeper they are fished, the better! Troll, still fish or cast, depending on conditions.

The strike of a big fish is liable to be harsh and sudden, especially to trolled bait. If still fishing, these fish will mouth the bait before taking it, but once they do, the action starts with a bang. Stay with it and hold on for dear life.

When landing either species remember they are big and strong, with a mouthful of razor-sharp teeth able to tear up the landing net in a single swipe and inflict mighty gashes on the fisherman's legs or hands. Club them over the head and shoot them if necessary. But make certain they're dead before reaching near the fish's mouth to extricate the hook. Use a long-handled hook-extractor or a pair of pliers.

Terminal tackle requirements are simple. Use adequate weights in the form of spoons and/or spinners ahead of the bait for casting or trolling with plastic-covered wire leaders to the hook.

Steelhead

This species of trout requires a different technique, terminal tackle, and bait than is customary under ordinary circumstances. Steelhead occupy the rivers of the Pacific Coast behind the salmon in a lusty quest for salmon eggs that have failed upstream spawning. Theirs is a constant diet of these eggs and as a result, they give little attention to other foods. Even when they can feed on other natural stream foods, these trout still prefer salmon eggs.

The salmon eggs drift down from above individually or in clus-ters, so it is up to the angler to duplicate this occurrence as best he can. Where salmon eggs are legal for use as bait, they are merely impaled on a very small hook as singles or doubles.

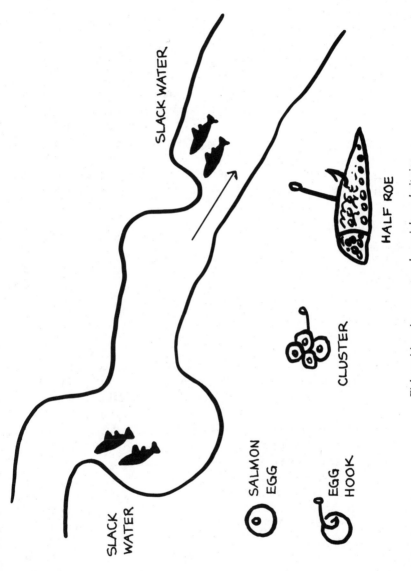

SLACK WATER

SLACK WATER

SALMON EGG

EGG HOOK

CLUSTER

HALF ROE

Fish positions in current and special egg bait rigs

Clusters of salmon eggs or, if not available, steelhead eggs can be used as shown.

Only during the season when salmon are absent will the resident steelhead take any interest at all in minnows or other baits. The standard standby is always mother earthworm, and it's best when all else fails.

Once hooked to a steelhead, the fisherman is in for some high jumps not unlike the kingly Atlantic salmon. He should be prepared for long runs and surface body rolls—keep his rod tip raised and the line as clear of obstructions as possible. For steelhead, always go equipped with sturdy tackle and plenty of reserve line. Fish for them from Northern California to British Columbia. These trout are plentiful in most coastal streams and the main trick is to be right there on the stream when a good "run" is on.

Stream Fishing Technique

The technique to use while fishing streams is primarily the "dead drift" method. If the bait merely hangs in the current unnaturally, it tends to spin to the surface. This is all right if the fish are very hungry, but for the bigger fish and those in heavily fished water, the closer the effect to natural drift of loose bait carried by the current, the better will be the results.

This means, when casting from shore or wading, that the cast should be made as shown in the accompanying illustrations in a quartering upstream direction, the path of the bait preplanned to drift down through a run—that is, by a rock, snag, into a deep hole or under an overhanging bank. In shallow streams where the current is fast, the bait will not sink rapidly unless slightly weighted; however, too much weight and there will be snagging. In deeper, slower water, weights should be kept to a minimum because slower current will allow the bait to drop down. Only in extremely fast water should heavy weights be used. The fisherman must learn by trial and error. He must develop his judgment and be willing to change weights to suit the problems at hand.

Basically, bait should drop as low to the bottom as possible without interruptions of drift caused by catching on the bottom. Shown here are some of the preferred sinkers and rigs. Note in some cases that a lighter strand of leader is used when the weight is at

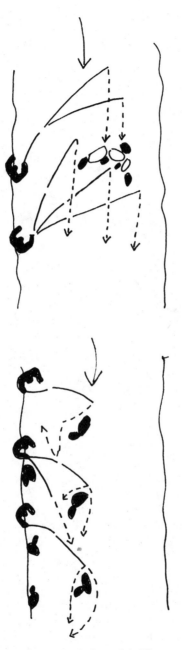

Two ways to work the rock holding water

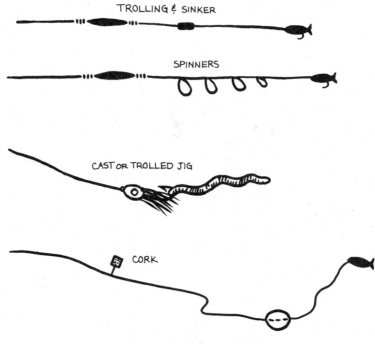

TROLLING & SINKER

SPINNERS

CAST OR TROLLED JIG

CORK

Four rigs for general fishing

the end of the line. This way, if the weight snags the bottom, the leader may break, losing the sinkers, but saving the rig.

The retrieve can and should be across the stream, across the main currents, and behind rocks and snags. The final reel-in should be slow since quite often fish will follow a bait around the circular retrieve and pounce on it only as it reaches the limit of its drift or as its retrieve is begun—often just as it is at the point of being whisked away.

Direct downstream baiting should be done by merely dropping the bait below the rod tip and allowing it to be tugged by the current. Where one can wade into the stream well above a rock or hot spot, and allow the bait to drift naturally down to the rock, this will appear as natural food drift to the fish. A good time for the fisherman to be prepared for a hefty strike!

Drift Fishing

This type of baiting can be done best by walking along the shore, the current stretch alongside, or from a boat controlled in its drift by oars, paddle or pole. Weights should be chosen that will get the bait down to the fish in a natural drift and not in a "pulled" position wherein the bait constantly tries to rise to the surface. In fishing from a boat, speed is the determining factor in depth and drift control.

As to the rig, some prefer the bait to drift *after* the weight, while others prefer it *before* the weight. Either way is satisfactory.

The fisherman casts to the side as far as he can and, if water-bound, has the boat held solidly for a moment while the bait tumbles through the current in a circular swing across the stream to the front and side of him respectively. The retrieve should be *very* slow in order to lure fish that may be following.

In very fash water, cast the rig on an upstream angle to cover more water and allow the bait to sink deeper.

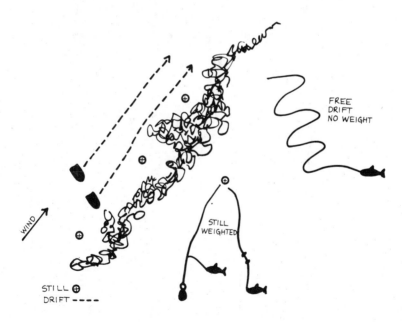

FREE
DRIFT
NO WEIGHT

STILL
WEIGHTED

WIND

STILL
DRIFT ----

Still and drift fishing suggestions and rigs

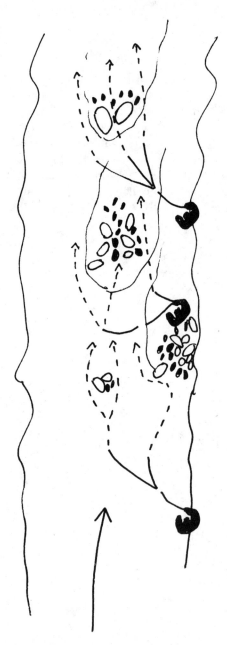

Positions and drifts for stream fishing

Drift fishing where the current carries the bait faster than the boat is truly the easiest to accomplish. Synchronize boat speed with current speed and the bait will drift beautifully into the holes and runs.

The rod is held flat to the water, but the drag is set to extremely light pressure. For the strike, the line should be cushioned. If the rod is held high, the bait tends to rise and remain on the surface.

Still Fishing

In this all one needs to do is locate a deep hole along the stream, a quiet water pocket in a bend or a long, quiet, slow stretch of water. Cast the bait and terminal rig into the water and let nature take its course. Allow the bait to sink down, but not snag the bottom.

Still fishing requires a soft-tipped rod for easy, short-distance casting. Terminal rigs are similar to those used in lake still fishing: one or two hooks on leaders (separated to avoid tangling) and a sinker. A slipping cork or bobber is set at a fixed position on the line, its proper place being measured to permit the bait a depth close to the bottom (directly *on* the bottom would risk a snag). Live worms, minnows or frogs are preferable baits since these swim around with satisfactory liveliness.

Another rig is the slip-sinker, with or without a bobber. As the fish pulls on the bait, the line slips through a hole in the sinker. This allows the fish a good long run before it is snubbed and it allows time to make sure that it has taken the bait securely.

Set the reel drag to light; prop the rod up on a forked stick and muse until something happens.

When a long rod is required in still fishing, use a 9-1/2 ft. fly rod equipped with either a closed-face spinning reel or a single-action fly reel. The old style cane pole system is outmoded and unnecessary for the one or two-rod angler.

Fishing conditions and fish species are more varied in streams than in lakes. But no two portions of a stream are the same, nor do they offer the same interesting situations. Game fish vary from the three favorite trout: brown, brook and rainbow; the bass: large and smallmouth; pickerel, perch, crappie, rock bass, walleye pike, northern pike, musky, catfish and carp. As seasons change, natural, aquatic, land-bred and unnatural baits can be used interchangeably. Their

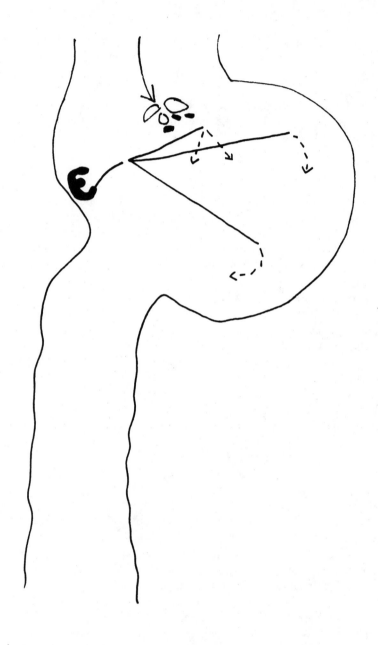

Fishing a side backwater

use is governed only by the angler's desire to catch and keep natural baits, coupled with the availability of such baits at the location.

One can fish streams by walking the shore or wading in the shallows. When wading broad streams or rivers, trustworthy chest-high waders are recommended. Fish all day, fish all night; the pleasures are constant and as fresh as the sport itself.

It is best for the angler to go equipped with terminal rigs prepared in advance, neatly coiled and labeled in the tackle box. This will save time on the water. Baits should be kept in containers that permit good ventilation and cool conditions. Hooks should be sharp and knots kept tied securely.

Bait fishing—especially in streams—is more interesting than artificial lure fishing inasmuch as this way the fisherman is offering the fish foods it likes, even though he may have to work a little in obtaining them. His tackle is geared for the task at hand, and this fishing demands a good caster who knows the proper techniques and manipulations so that the fish will look upon his bait offerings as entirely natural, convenient, attractive, and without suspicion.

Saltwater Bait Fishing

Saltwater bait fishing can be divided into three basic categories. It is done from the shore, casting from the beach, rocks, jetties and mudflats. Casting, trolling and stillfishing are done from boats in protected bays and inlets, outlets, inland waterways and coves. Offshore trolling is done on the open ocean, near the oceanic shelves, drop-offs, reefs and islands.

You do not need to own a boat. There are party boats, where as many as a hundred anglers join together for half-day, or full-day trips to the fishing grounds. Take one of these excursions and anglers will be seen fishing with varied types of equipment and using many diversified techniques for catching fish. Small boats and motors can be rented for bay fishing. More expensive craft can be "chartered" complete with captain and first mate for a trip offshore in search of the big prizes. Generally four to six anglers can chip in and charter one of these boats for half-day, full-day or as long as desired, all depending on what vacation time and wallet permit. In party boats and charter boats, the bait and—in some instances—the tackle are supplied, including guidance on how to use them by the crew. This is, incidentally, often compulsory since the reputation of the boat and crew depends upon their patrons catching fish, hence they wish to maintain their image as guides "par excellence."

TIDES

The biggest natural difference found in the ocean that does not exist in lakes or most rivers is the tide. Every six hours the ocean's water "rises" and every six hours it "falls." In some areas like the Bay of Fundy between Upper Maine and New Brunswick, the tide rises more than forty feet—quite a change! In other parts of the world, such as in the Bahamas, the change amounts to only a few feet.

This constant action keeps life in the ocean moving in a continually predictable routine. The fisherman who knows the schedule of natural events can plan his strategy accordingly and, depending on fish migrations and the movement of bait fish, be assured of catching enough fish to fill his freezer.

This tidal action affects everything from the amount of water to the minutest form of life, including the bait upon which the resident of roving fish feed. As the tide comes into a bay, for example, clams, worms and other forms of food liven up. The minnows begin to feed and form schools. The bigger fish move in from deeper water searching for them. When the tide is on the rise, it is a good time to fish, particularly near the "top" of the tide. But in many cases an equally good time can be had on the "ebb" of the tide. Thus, when the current is falling, it brings the bait fish down out of the inlets and away from the coves and into the channels. Big fish know this and wait there for them. Learn the subleties of tide action in relation to the wind and its effect on bait and sport fish.

TROLLING TECHNIQUES

Trolling and certain drift fishing are effective for weakfish or sea trout, jacks, redfish and a host of other worthy fishes. Drifting along on the current, one can cover much more territory than the

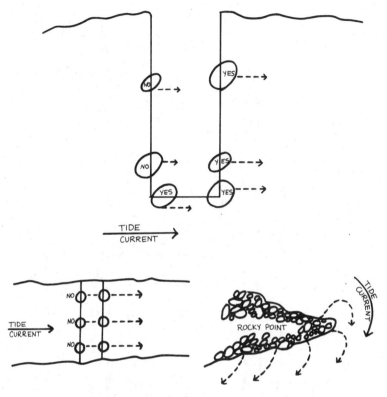

How to fish from the dock and the leeside of a point of land

anchored fisherman, and be apt to encounter more varied fish species. The trolling rig is a mere variation of the bottom rig of conventional terminal tackle. Use enough swivels and check for weeds, or else the line will tangle unmercifully. Don't try to work line that's too long; 100 feet is enough. Try to hold the boat in a nearly stationary position in the tide; allow the current to do the actual trolling. At other times, drift with the current and the line will actually be "still fished" while moving along.

In the case of casting live shrimp or cut bait, one can cast ahead of his drift; allow the baits to sink and the bobber to float the works along a mangrove shore or edge of rocks, varying boat speed and position to the current and size of area being fished.

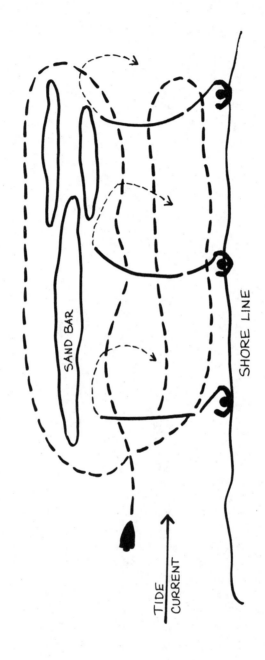

Fishing the outer sand bar

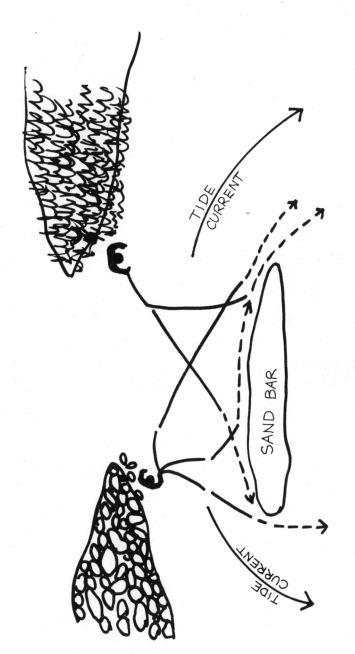

TIDE
CURRENT

SAND BAR

TIDE
CURRENT

Fishing the outer sand bar from beach or from points of shore reef

Most bottom fish dislike strong current. A good trolling time to pick is the slack of the tide, or just as the tide hits the low or begins the rise, or just before and immediately after high tide. The high is generally the better of the two, and far superior to a "running tide" for this kind of fishing. When the tide is flowing fast, drift and troll with it. Work the points of land, rocky ledges and reefs, yes—but don't neglect the sandy bays and especially the muddy sections, particularly if fishing for flounders. Go aboard for a day's trip on a party boat. It is quite educational.

SURF, BEACH AND JETTY FISHING

One active step up from fishing for the little bottom fish of bays and coves is the sport of jetty, surf and beach fishing: casting and trolling for the more energetic varieties. Bluefish up to ten pounds can be and are taken from these vantages. They come in with the tide, rushing schools of bait. As they surge by and spot cut bait, they'll hit it. Same for striped bass, pollock, jacks, mackerel, snook and tarpon, not to mention channel bass, shark and many more species. In between these runs—nothing but bait stealers. Sometimes one will fish almost an entire tide and enjoy peak fishing only for a matter of a few minutes. It's a waiting game, but well worth it.

Tide and wind are the prime considerations. When the fish are "in," the best times for jetty and beach fishing are at the upturn of the tide from low, and again at high to an hour or so after, night or day. Consider the wind direction and try to locate a position for casting with the wind rather than against it.

For the smaller fish, use cut bait, clams, sea worms and crabs, but when the stripers and blues are in, for example, whole bait fish or crabs that can be cast a good distance are best.

If these cannot be acquired, cut bait will still suffice. Whole or cut squid are often used by night fishermen as are eel skins attached to specially weighted hook rigs. These last are good for fishing canals or in fishing from bridges and jetties.

For the surf, whole bait fish, squid, shrimp or any cut bait such as clams, strips of flesh from caught fish, etc., will be quite sufficient.

Wind direction and force may be much against the fisherman. If so, he may find himself up against the old problem of trying to figure out how to get the heavy bait a good distance out and away from him without having the wind drop it near his feet. Therefore, never go under-tackled for this sport; conditions under which casting may have to be done coupled with the potential power of a hooked fish suggest the angler should rather go over-tackled than under. A big bluefish, tarpon or striper can give more than the fisherman bargained for. Learn to cast with accuracy and as far out as possible without line snags and hang-ups. Bring a lot of terminal tackle since bottom snags will happen often, and also be sure to bring an over-supply of bait.

The bait should be kept frozen and in a container that will preserve it as long as possible. Keep it out of the sun. If live bait is used, sink the bait can or cage underwater, tie it securely to a rock and watch the tide level. Watch the relationship between wind, tide and barometer, keeping alert for quick changes.

Depending on the season, dress accordingly. The night fisherman should make sure everything is in its right place, available by touch. Again, keep an eye on the weather. It would be a shame to miss good fishing just because of forgetting to bring the proper clothing, food or other necessities.

Trolling Beach and Jetty

It would seem better to be out in a boat for fishing a jetty or beach with more efficiency. Over the years, however, one will find that whether in a boat or fishing from the land, both methods will produce. Also, quite often, waves and weather prohibit all but the brave (and sometimes the too-daring) fishermen from boat fishing. Rough water and fierce winds can be too much to bear even if there is some possible shelter in the lee of protruding rocks. Still it is in such weather, particularly in northern areas, that the fishing may be tops.

The troller has the theoretical advantage of being able to cover more fishing territory in less time than the angler who wanders up and down the beach or clambers over the rough rocks of a jetty. Certainly, ''fish hunting'' is better done by trolling. Casting from the shore is more of a waiting game. To troll successfully the angler must always be aware of the tide, how each hour affects the local waters, how the currents bring in the bait, how the wind crosses up

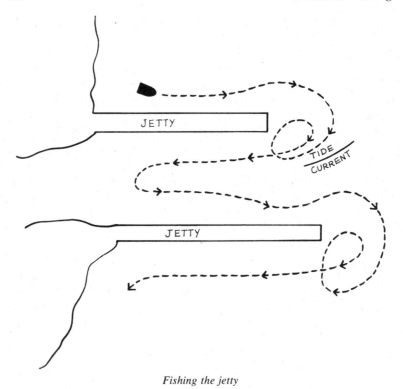

Fishing the jetty

the surface of the water. Watch the sky for the presence of sea gulls feeding on the surface, for this signifies action underwater. The big fish are schooling up the bait, driving them to the surface and the gulls are snatching their share. Also watch for approaching squalls.

Trolling rigs are basically simple. Drift trolling can also involve using the bobber and is particularly effective alongside a jetty right in the mouth of an inlet. Drift fishing is also productive near the surf when a long pool of water inside a sandbar is seen to contain roving big fish chasing smaller ones swept into the "pool."

If the bottom is full of rocks, try to keep the bait above them by adjusting the weight-boat-speed ratio. If the bottom is sandy, troll deeper.

Most jetty and beach trolling is done from relatively small boats. This argues for keeping a sharp "weather eye" peeled. As to the tackle, set the reel drag to well under the breaking strain of the line. Tighten it later after a strike. When fishing whole bait fish it is best to allow the line free drag so the game fish has time to mouth it a bit. Then when he has decided to run with it—strike!

Never troll with the rod unattended. Even if it is set into the rod holder, make sure that everything is free, that the line is always uncaught in the guides and that other gear aboard is well away from sudden action. If the rod is hand-held, make sure fingers are well away from the line. Set the reel's antireverse so that the handle will not spin on strike or in case the weights become snagged. If two lines are being trolled and a fish hits one of them, the other must be reeled in quickly to avoid a possibly bad tangle. Have the net or gaff ready and the oars and other gear out of action's way.

While fighting a fish, keep a watch so that the boat is not carried into a dangerous tide rip, or pushed up on a rock ledge. Keep alert for other boats. They should keep their distance, but don't depend on it. Watch also for heavy wakes from any passing boats.

If two are fishing, one can man the motor and guide the boat according to the conditions. Then they can take turns fishing.

The training acquired here fishing along the shore is a good rehearsal for the big game show to be experienced out on the open ocean, well offshore and away from the safety of sheltered waters.

OFFSHORE TROLLING FOR BIG GAME FISH

This is big time angling for glamour fish found in ocean depths. Some anglers consider it less sporting and less fun than fighting smaller fish on lighter tackle—a bonefish a greater thrill than a 700-pound tuna, for example. But others are consumed with the idea of breaking world records and love the idea of battling a powerful fish three times their weight for hours on end.

Still, good choices can be found fishing for lightweights of this kind in offshore fishing and the heavies. Offshore fishing does not necessarily mean that all the fish have to be big. There is plenty of fun and sport, for instance, in catching a 20-pound king mackerel on 5-pound test line with medium weight freshwater spinning rod and reel. And it will take time and skill to boat it; the same is true for a 35-pound sailfish or wahoo. There's plenty of thrill also in taking a 40-pound school tuna on light tackle, perhaps more so with light gear than in taking a 700–pounder with the winch-like tackle required for such giants of the sea.

Striped bass, bluefish, cobia, amberjack and, off the Pacific Coast, the yellowtail and several species of smaller tuna will fill the small-to-intermediate bill for deep water light tackle fishing. The big bottom fish, like the jewfish or grouper, will run up to 200 pounds. Catching them offers much long-term steady pull. When it comes to shark, that's something else again. Here the fisherman is up against brawn, tenacity and more excitement than some anglers ever find with the big black, blue-and-white marlin or giant bluefins. So the choice is wide and so are the methods.

Equipment-wise, gear can vary from heavy freshwater items to the heaviest of the saltwater gear complete with a fighting chair in a cruiser cockpit. Boat-wise, it varies from using a twin-engined outboard skiff for quick runs out and back to luxurious 26-foot to over 40-foot cruisers.

Rented outboards and inboards can be obtained at most coastal fishing centers by the day, week or month—even by the entire season. Many anglers who want to fish during a great deal of their vacation period hire a guide and his craft for the whole time.

The formal charter boats are the big ones for long, fast, safe trips to waters well offshore. These craft are seaworthy and capable of operating through storms and sudden blows. Many are equipped with cabins where all necessities and meals can be served. They have plenty of cockpit space for action. The catch is iced and cleaned, or may be turned over to the captain, unless of trophy significance.

Terminal Tackle for Offshore Fishing

Use bottom tackle or trolling and drifting tackle as usual and slightly heavier tackle if after the big fish. The difference in this kind of fishing from that of the inshore variety is that most trolling will be done with the baits riding directly on the ocean surface.

In most cases, with the exception of trolling for bluefish and stripers in their class, the baits are kept up on the surface but out of the boat's wake by outriggers—long poles angled outward from the craft. Once the terminal rig is set up, the fishing line is attached by means of a clothespin to another line extending over a small pulley at the top of the outrigger and down to the cockpit. By this means the fishing line is then hoisted so that it extends from the reel to the top of the outrigger. The cruiser is started and the baits are allowed to drift and skip along the ocean surface as the boat moves along at appropriate trolling speed. When a fish strikes, the line is jerked from the clothespin and the fisherman's battle is underway. Until this happens, he can do but little except sit, watch, wait and hope. There's a thrill in seeing a marlin, for example, as it approaches sometimes from way behind the bait. He sneaks up on it, makes several passes at it, etc., before finally coming in for the kill.

Rigging the bait to the hook for this kind of fishing is an art that few anglers ever learn or really need to learn. The bait, be it a bonefish, bluefish, or a lesser species such as the flying fish, is opened up, the backbone removed in most cases, and the hook is sewed into the fish in such a way that it will remain vertical when towed as bait. It will flash and wobble more naturally this way and must not be allowed to spin on the line. Those big fish are very choosey!

Other baits are cut fish for drifting and bottom fishing, squid, or strips of most any fish available.

Much of deep sea sport fishing and trolling involves chumming. Before setting out for the fishing area, the boat is loaded with several containers of mashed-up menhaden, herring or other bait or trash fish, including the innards of dead sport fish mashed to form an oily, stew-like mess. When the fishing grounds are reached and the course, current and drift are established, the mate scoops out dipper-fulls of the chumming bait, tossing them overboard at regular intervals in the hope of drawing fish to the area and the trolled baits. Hence the anglers fish in the chumming "slick." In general, chumming is effective and widely-practiced in offshore fishing. It has been virtually traditional in deep sea fishing for many, many decades; for that matter, perhaps even for centuries.

Equipping for Big Game Fishing

First comes the boat—a cabin cruiser of from 28 to 40 or more feet—twin-engined; plenty of cockpit space; a forward cabin for rest and shelter; and electronic equipment for safety and depth-finding.

Then the tackle is aboard for whatever species is sought. Fighting chairs are needed, usually a pair mounted on the floor of the cockpit. These revolve in a circle somewhat like a barber chair so the angler is always in line with his fish. (When the boat needs to be moved still further in any direction, the skipper, watching the show from his perch above the cabin roof, makes the necessary angulations and speed changes.) The fighting chair has a circular hole for the rod butt. The fisherman wears a harness (of which there are several versions) which can be fastened to each side of the reel. In fighting a large fish, this helps distribute the strain to back and shoulders, as well as arms and legs. The rod holders are usually mounted on the sides of the gunwales and are used for storage and also in fishing if more than the chair rods are used at the same time.

A flying gaff is a very necessary instrument and its barb is to be sunk home into the fish when the mate grasps the leader with his gloved hands preparatory to landing the fish. An assortment of nylon lines (ropes) are needed sometimes to put a loop around the head and tail of the fish, especially if it is a billfish or shark. As stated, a flying bridge or tuna tower is a necessity when trying to locate and later maneuver the boat when a giant is on the line. From his elevated position up there the skipper can see over the swells or chops and survey the water for quite a long distance when seeking fish. Outriggers, bait storage cans for bait and chum, long-handle and heavy-duty gaff and gin pole are needed, the last serving often in towing or hoisting a large trophy.

Fishing Tackle and Terminal Gear

Since interest runs high with both skippers and anglers for trophy and prize-winning fish, contest regulations applicable to big game fishing and tackle are closely adhered to by all deepwater salts. Some lucky fisherman might hook into a big prizewinner or world's record fish the first time out, and it would be a pity if his tackle were not "regulation." Of course, it is not necessarily the biggest fish that counts, but the biggest taken on specifically weighted and measured gear. This is all set up by the International Game Fish Association, a worldwide clearing house for records.

The big game reels used are marked in sizes from 1/0 to 6/0. They are manufactured by excellent companies such as Ocean City,

Penn, Fin-Nor and Garcia, to mention but a few. These are perfectly designed for heavy fast-running and jumping fish. They are built to stand off terrific pressures.

Lines and their capacities as recommended by the manufacturer are based on thread sizes as previously mentioned. The I.G.F.A. recognizes only 3, 6, 9, 15, 24, 39 and 54-thread lines and their strengths are judged when wet. Experts agree that braided nylon or dacron is just about impervious to deterioration in salt water, but these lines do have a good deal of stretch, some more than others, which is a hindrance in some situations. On a long line, their hooking qualities, due to this stretch, are less predictable than is the case with linen lines.

Rods also have a system of classification according to the weight of the tip section. They range from 4 to 36 ounces. For example, take the combination of a correctly balanced set-up. A 9/12 outfit requires a rod with a tip of 9 ounces which will work best with 12-thread line testing at 36 pounds. For such a combination, the correct reel for most conditions will be a 4/0.

Suggested Balanced Tackle Combos

It would be quite impossible and unnecessary to catalogue each and every well-balanced tackle combination here, but five have been selected to cover the range of sizes deemed most practicable.

16/24 Heavy Tackle

Rod: 6 feet, 9 inches overall length.
Tip: Not less than 5 feet. Weight, 16 ounces.
Line: 24-thread, 72 pounds, wet.
Leader: 15-foot length; nor limit re strength.
Reel: No restrictions; usually 4/0 to 9/0.

9/18 Medium Tackle

Rod: Length 6 1/2 feet.
Tip: 5 feet. Weight, 9 ounces.
Line: 18 thread, 54 pounds, wet.
Leader: 15 foot; no weight restrictions.
Reel: Usually 4/0 to 6/0.

6/9 Light Tackle

Rod: 6 feet.
Tip: Not less than 5 feet. Weight 6 ounces.
Butt: 18 inches.
Line: 9-thread, 27 pounds, wet.
Leader: 15-foot; no strength restrictions.
Reel: Usually 3/0 to 4/0.

4/6 Light Tackle

Rod: 6 feet.
Tip: Not less than 5 feet, weight 4 ounces.
Butt: Length, 18 inches.
Line: 6-thread, 18 pounds, wet.
Leader: 15-foot; no test restriction.
Reel: Usually 2/0 or 3/0.

3/6 Light Tackle

Rod: 6 feet including butt; 6 ounces in all.
Tip: 5 feet in length.
Butt: 12 inches.
Line: 6-thread, 18 pounds, wet.
Leader: 15-foot: no weight restriction.
Reel: 2/0 or 3/0.

Hooks

Certainly there is a specific hook which is best suited because of its design for certain species of fish and made in size that will capture them properly.
Sailfish: O'Shaughnessy 7/0 to 9/0.
School Tuna: 20 to 45 pounds. Sobey 7/0, 40 to 100 pounds; 8/0 or 9/0, O'Shaughnessy.

Check the I.G.F.A. records occasionally for changes in tackle specifications and record fish recorded.

Shark Fishing

The surf, jetty and even the bay fisherman will encounter sharks when least expected. It is fun when even a supposedly docile sand shark takes hold. The fight is not dramatic, but there will be a lot of pulling and hauling before the fish is exhausted. These are "accident" sharks, the same as those often hooked through chance out on the big deep. Quite often while trolling for anything from offshore striped bass, school tuna or the big marlin and tuna, a shark will be hooked. Chances are, if it is big, it will eventually get away, since hooks used for ordinary game fish will not suffice. The leaders also, being of wire rather than chain, will not always hold a big one.

Sharks will also attack hooked big game fish. They are attracted to the thrashing of the game fish on the hook and, as the fish tires, they move in for the kill—sometimes as many as six or eight of them. Quite often this leaves the fisherman with only the head of his hooked fish, the shark having taken the most of it and departed. Many world's records have been lost this way.

There is, however, the specialized sport of shark fishing. In this, the fisherman deliberately tackles up for the monsters, using the heaviest rod available and the biggest reel with the strongest lines. Then he attaches a shark chain "leader" and a proper hook of a type described earlier. But before leaving for shark fishing, it's necessary to visit the meat market or a meat processing plant to obtain gallons of blood. Fish chum, animal guts and meat are useful, too. Quite a makings for the shark's dinner! Once out on the ocean, the sharking specialist starts his chum line, sets his baits in the outriggers, and the day starts. Other necessary equipment includes nylon lines—ropes for looping the head and tail of the shark when it is about to be boated. The boat should have a gin pole, a stout pole attached to the side of the boat, aft of the cabin, but not in the way of open deck areas where fish are hauled aboard. The shark will eventually be lashed to this pole if it is too large to haul aboard otherwise.

Now, a shark unceremoniously takes hold of the bait. Marlin and other fish usually will first follow the bait for a while, being very touchy and aware that it just might not be to their liking. The shark, on the other hand, throws caution to the wind, since he is virtual king of the sea. His strike is not especially shattering. He merely grabs the bait and takes off the moment he hooks himself, unless the fisherman has already set the hook. Most sharks do not do a great deal of jumping, but the hammerhead and the blue are known to go in for surface acrobatics.

Battling a shark can be long and laborious, but it will rarely be as quiet and long-pull a tussle as in the case of the bluefin tuna. When the shark is tired out, the mate readies the flying gaff, clears the deck for action, readies his lines for the loops. As the shark swims by and if the mate assesses it as thoroughly tired, he attempts to place a loop, first over the snout of the shark, and then one over the tail. In the meantime, the fisherman stays in the fighting chair, doing his part. Quite often several tries will go by, the shark merely swimming by for a closer look.

But when the right time comes, the loops are made secure and the gaff driven into its mark. Finally the shark is led around to the gin pole where, by various means devised by the skipper, it is made fast. It's quite a fight!

A word of warning! Don't look for shark trouble unless from a big seaworthy boat that's properly equipped and manned with at least one person who really knows what he is doing! This is a dangerous sport. Sharks have been known to jump right into the cockpit of a boat. If the boat is small, such as an offshore open skiff, they can bash in the transom or smash the rudder and propeller. Once aboard, that seemingly docile shark can come quickly to life and tear up the deck and everything on it. They don't seem to die very fast, even when shot. Actually, there seems to be no proved way to dispatch them promptly and efficiently.

So, don't go out as a tyro adventurer and tangle with sharks. It takes a great deal of knowhow. Despite this, sharking can be a real he-man sport with greater appeal to some than fishing for the usual big game fish. There are even charter skippers who specialize in this sport.

But, until the new shark fisherman has accompanied an experienced one a few times, he won't really have the knowledge and experience as to what is actually needed for the safety of the boat, the equipment and other people on board, should he be tempted to try it on his own.

PART THREE

Fish of Most Interest to Sportsmen

The northern hemisphere is blessed with hundreds of beautiful, hard-fighting, good-eating species of sport and food fish. To appreciate this great heritage, conservation should be an ethic vital to every sport and recreational fisherman.

FRESHWATER SPECIES

The popularity of freshwater fishing is certainly not confined to those living only in inland states. As a matter of fact, four of the ten states listed several years ago as having the largest number of fishing license sales were states where saltwater fishing was also available. So let's look at six categories of freshwater species that offer so much fishing fun to so many anglers.

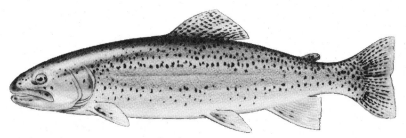

Rainbow trout

The Trouts

Six major species of trout inhabit the brooks, streams and lakes of our northern countryside and Canada. The brook trout, actually a char (Salvelinus fontinalis), once native of New England, has become widely distributed across the map. One-half to two-pounders make a good meal and a record-breaker may even range to five pounds.

The rainbow (Salmo gairdneri), cutthroat (Salmo clarki), and steelhead, sea-run rainbow, are essentially West Coast and West-of-the-Mississippi species. The rainbow has been introduced into Eastern waters and is now considered "native." Good catches range from five to twenty-five pounds.

The brown trout (Salmo trutta) is an import from Europe and, since 1880, a naturalized citizen, ranging in size from one to twenty-five pounds and more.

Brown trout

Lake trout

All these species feed on aquatic stream and lake insects, minnows and blow-ins and are taken in legal season by a variety of tackle.

The lake trout (Salvelinus namaycush), similar to the brook trout, is somewhat larger and is found mainly in northern lakes.

Pacific Salmons

All of these salmon, the coho (Oncorhynchus kisutch), the chinook (Oncorhynchus tshawytscha) and the sockeye (Onchorhynchus nerka), are ocean inhabitants of the Pacific Northwest and Alaska, ascending the rivers and streams to spawn. While in salt water, they are trolled and cast for in the bays as they approach the spawning rivers. Bait fish are trolled, usually in combination with spoons and

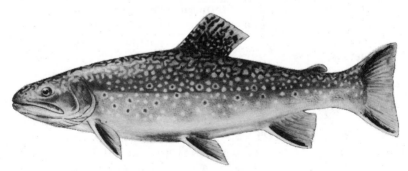

Brook trout

spinners to attract them. Bait fishing is not done, however, once these fish are in the true stream. Other salmon, the Atlantic and the landlocked of northeastern waters, are rarely taken on bait, and fly-fishing only is the rule for Atlantics. Powerful jumpers and long runners, they offer kingly sport in their ten to fifty-pound range. Spinning gear and baitcasting tackle are used and trolling is of the shallow variety. The salmon is a best-rated food fish.

Freshwater Basses

Two common species are represented in the large bass family in our fresh waters. They are the largemouth bass (Micropterus salmoides), and the smallmouth bass (Micropterus dolomieui). They are similar in shape and markings, though the smallmouth is a bit slimmer and more bronze. The relative position of the upper jaw and the eye help to identify the differences between the species.

A good catch of largemouths would range from three to ten pounds, larger in the Deep South; the smallmouth would be big at six pounds. Primarily lake and slow stream species, they are also found in faster rivers and brooks that enter into or empty from large lakes and impoundments. Their basic food is anything that moves, from mice to frogs, small birds to minnows and aquatic insects. They are taken on fly, spin and bait casting tackle.

Northern Pike, Muskellunge and Walleye Pike

These two species, the northern pike (Esox lucius) and the muskellunge (Esox masquingy), are our two largest species of game fish. They are quite similar in shape, varying in skin markings and head details. They are found only in the more northern states and Canada, and have not been introduced as widely as the trouts and basses.

Their food is similar to the basses', but due to their larger size, they eat larger minnows, other game and food fish, aquatic insects, birds, mice and frogs. These are fierce fighters and heavy tackle is needed. Trolling is the most popular method and in the summertime, deep trolling is what gets them. A big pike will range from fifteen to twenty-five pounds and a prize musky will go to forty pounds.

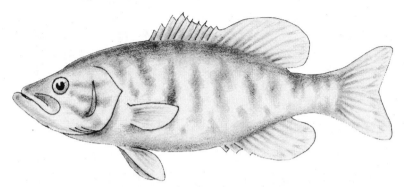

Smallmouth bass

The walleye pike (Stizostedion vitreum) looks like a combination of a pike and a perch. The specie is a trifle smaller than the northern pike and the muskellunge and not a strong battler. The walleye usually ranges from five to ten pounds, but many are caught each summer weighing far more.

The walleye is prized as a tasty food fish.

The chain pickerel (Esox niger), found in lakes and slow rivers, is another smaller version of the pike, usually ranging from two to five pounds, although many are taken well over these weights. The pickerel is a fierce fighter on light tackle.

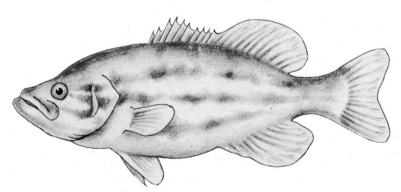

Largemouth bass

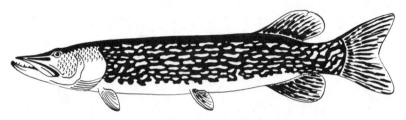

Northern pike

General Panfish

In the perch family, yellow (Perca flavescens), and white (Roccus americanus), the crappie family, white (Pomoxis annularis), and black (Pomoxis nigromaculatus) are our most common species. The sunfish family includes the bluegill sunfish (Lepomis macrochirus) and the several varieties of smaller species. All are found in most waters, particularly through the Central United States and the Southland. They are small, plentiful and full of fight for their size. They are energetic feeders, particularly on surface baits. Their diet consists of aquatic and blow-in insects and small minnows. Gear of the ultra-light category is best used to enjoy these splashing, spunky little fighters. They range in size from one-half pound to three pounds.

Other Panfish

Included in this category, for convenience and brevity, are several species which are only "unofficially" considered game fish, since they do offer fun on light tackle. The catfish family is a large one, with the blue (Ictalurus melas), and the channel (Ictalurus punc-

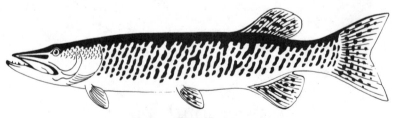

Muskellunge

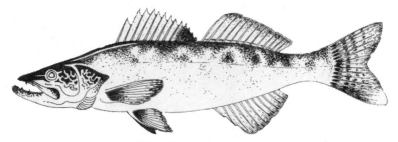

Walleye pike

tatus) the principal and larger cats. The carp (Cyprinus carpio) belongs to the "goldfish" family. The suckers, another large family, are represented by several species, the lake chubsucker (Erimyzon sucetta) having the widest distribution. They are all bottom feeders and their diet ranges from aquatic vegetation and man-made concoctions of smelly baits, fish or insects, as in the case of the catfish. The channel catfish grows to forty pounds in the large rivers and carp will weigh from four to forty pounds. Suckers and fallfish in their myriad variations range up to two or three pounds. All can be taken on light to medium freshwater tackle and appropriate baits.

SALTWATER SPECIES

Striped, Channel Bass and Seabass

Three of the most popular of the large saltwater bass family, the striped bass (Roccus saxatilis), channel bass (Sciaenops ocellatus) and sea bass of many species, are found on both coasts. The

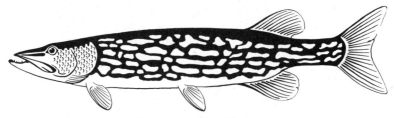

Chain pickerel

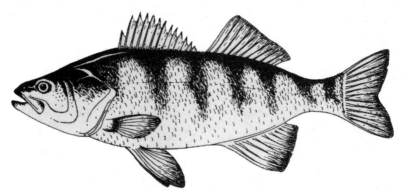

Yellow perch

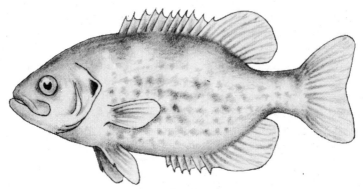

Rock bass

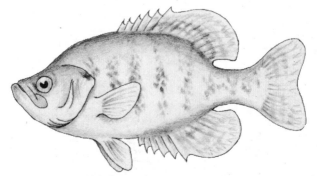

White crappie

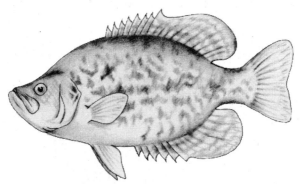

Black crappie

Redbreast sunfish

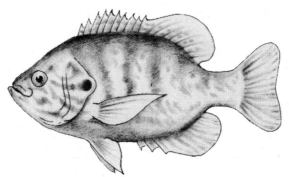

Bluegill sunfish

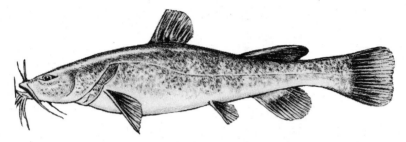

Flathead catfish

striped bass were introduced to the state of Oregon from the East. They range along the shore, not being found in the open ocean in company with marlins and tunas. They are semi-anadromous, often spawning in the brackish waters of inlets and river outlets that afford easy escape from saltwater. Their food consists of the shellfish, aquatic life of all kinds including shrimp, school bait fish, shellfish, crabs and sea worms. They are fished (depending on seasonal conditions) from the bottom to the top with the exception of the sea bass which remain in deep waters most of the year. Trolling and casting is done along the shore for stripers and channel bass, but bottom fishing is recommended for the numerous species of sea bass.

They range in weight from three to fifty pounds. California black sea bass (Stereolepis gigas) range up to two hundred pounds.

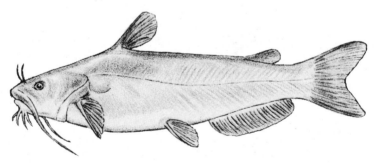

White catfish

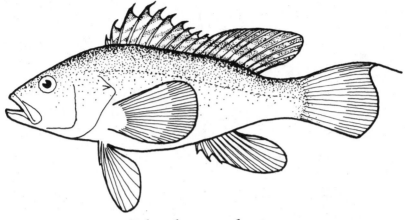

Black sea bass

Pollock, Cod and Bluefish

These three species are grouped here for the purposes of re-
gional and similar fishing considerations rather than by category.
They are limited in range to the East Coast: the pollock (Pollachius
virens) and cod (Gadus callarias) ranging from Newfoundland to
Cape Cod; the bluefish (Pomatomus saltratrix) ranging from Cape
Cod to Florida. The pollock is essentially a bottom fish similar to

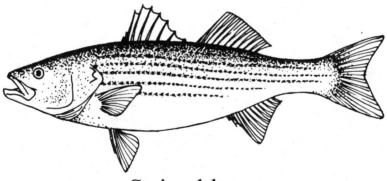

Striped bass

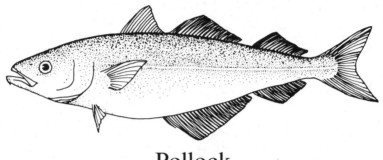

Pollock

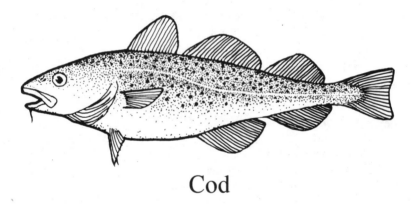

Cod

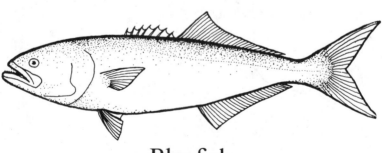

Bluefish

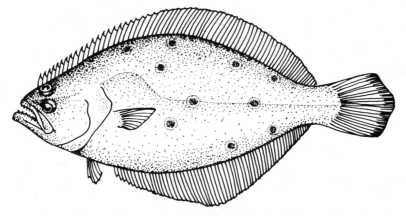

Summer flounder

the cod, yet unlike the cod, it is found in the spring and fall along beaches and points of land, feeding on roving schools of bait fish in company with the bluefish and striped bass. The cod remains out in the deep ocean and is a favorite of partyboat anglers and those who like to bounce their sinkers on the bottom. Striped bass and bluefish afford much sport to anglers fishing from the beach, jetties and points of land. They usually cast or troll for them mostly in the tide rips, inlets and river mouths. All manner of light to heavy tackle is used

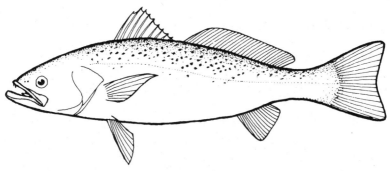

Weakfish

and bait consists of crustaceans, shrimp, squid, sand or sea worms and school bait fish common at the scene. Strong fighters, these denizens of the briny blue range in size from three to forty pounds.

Saltwater Panfish, Flounders, Porgies, etc.

The *et cetera* includes skates and a half-hundred species of bottom fish found in bays, inlets, beaches, mudflats and rocky bottoms, inshore and offshore. The Atlantic halibut is a large flounder or fluke weighing up to four hundred pounds. There are simply too many of these species to cover in a single book, the summer flounder (Paralichthys dentatus) and the porgie, known as the scaup (Stenotomus chrysops) and the sheepshead (Archosargus probatocephalus) being the most common. Variations of all are found on both coasts, being caught frequently by trolling, but mostly by bottom fishing. The flounders inhabit sandy and muddy bottoms, while the porgies are found in sandy and rocky bottoms and around old wrecks. Flounders range in weight from one to four pounds, the porgies up to twenty pounds. Food consists of crustaceans, crabs, worms, and small fish. Light to medium tackle is used, except in cases of giant halibut.

Weakfish and Sea Trout

These two species are quite similar in markings, size and shape. They feed on crustaceans, small bait fish, sea worms, shrimp and cut bait. The common weakfish of northern waters (Cynoscion regalis) ranges from Cape Cod to Maryland, while the spotted sea trout or weakfish (Cynoscion nebulosus) ranges from Florida and around the Gulf Coast into Texas and Mexico. Both are considered tops in food value and offer sport in the inshore estuaries, inlets, bays, and inland waterways. They are found in brackish waters. They are similar in shape to the freshwater trout with the exception of the extended dorsal fin. They are sporty, even when small, if fished on light tackle, and are favorites with bridge, jetty, beach and small boat anglers. Light saltwater and light freshwater tackle can be used. Weakfish range in size from one to five pounds and the spotted sea trout can go as high as ten pounds or better.

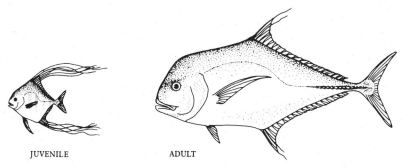

JUVENILE   ADULT

African pompano

Pompano, Jack, Permit and Amberjack

This family of fish has many species, only the most popular of which are included here. The common pompano (Trachinotus carolinus) along with the round and long fin are found from Cape Hattaras to the entire range of outer islands; Cuba and around the Florida peninsula along the Gulf Coast. Pompano bait includes cut fish, sand fleas, plus numerous crustaceans, crabs and shrimp. The common jack (Caranx hippos) along with the horse-eye, blue runner and yellow are similar in habitat and diet. They range in weight from five to ten pounds. The great amberjack (Seriola zonata) is found in deep water from New Jersey to the West Indies and specimens range

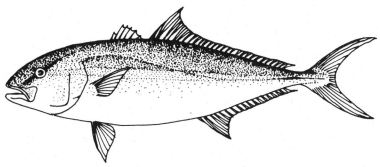

Greater amberjack

Snook

to over one hundred pounds. Warm waters, offshore flats, reefs and wrecks are its habitat. Big gear is needed here to keep this one from fouling a fishing line on the bottom.

Snook and Tarpon

These two gamesters will truly test tackle and angling skill. Found from Georgia to the Florida peninsula and along the Gulf Coast to Mexico, they offer sport to millions of light and medium-tackle anglers. The snook (Centropomus undecimalis) resembles the cod in shape but not in action. Found near and in inshore waters, bays, inlets, protected waterways and especially among the man-

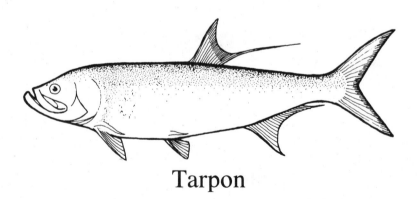

Tarpon

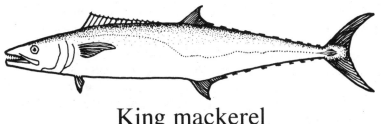

King mackerel

groves, both the snook and the tarpon (Tarpon atlanticus) feed on shrimp, mullet and other bait fish. Snook run to thirty pounds and while tarpon run smaller in the rivers and estuaries, they're caught as big as one hundred and fifty pounds to as high as two hundred pounds. Taken by trolling, still fishing and casting, both species are worth the effort and will provoke tall tale telling. Tarpon are not good table fare, but snook are cookbook classics.

Boston, Spanish and King Mackerel

Boston mackerel (Scomber scombrus) range from Newfoundland to Cape Hattaras and are prized as a food fish but considered small as gamesters go, reaching only four pounds. The Spanish mackerel (Scomberomorus maculatus) grows twice the size and inhabits warmer waters, as in the tropics. Both are school fish and the angler can catch a bucketful in a few minutes. Bits of fish flesh,

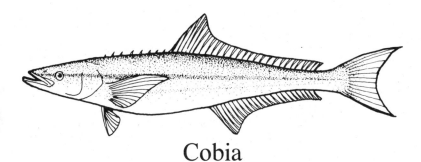

Cobia

shrimp or beach minnows are best baits. Small freshwater tackle, even fly rods, are used.

The king mackerel (Scomberomorus cavalla) are much larger and taken regularly up to one hundred pounds. At times they are found inshore accompanied by the Spanish mackerel, but more frequently they are in offshore waters with dolphin and sailfish. Big tackle needed here and baits are those used for general big game fish: mackerel, bonefish, mullet.

Bonefish, Ladyfish

The bonefish (Albula vulpes) is the fastest running fish when hooked and held. Taken in the shallows of South Florida, the Bahamas and outer islands, the hooked fish has only one way to go and that's to the wide open sea, where it heads with alarming power and speed. Heavy fly tackle, spinning gear and light-tipped rods and heavy-duty bait casting reels with at least one hundred yards of backing are needed. The bait can be conch, shrimp, crabs or bits of fish depending on the circumstances. These fish weigh from six to nine pounds.

The ladyfish (Elops saurus) is similar in appearance though not as fast as the bonefish. It's found in similar circumstances when in on the broad flats from the deep to feed. It weighs up to ten pounds.

Tuna, Albacore and Bonito

This is a big family with fish widely ranging in size from ten to seven hundred pounds. The big game angler knows the bluefin tuna (Thunnus thynus) on sight due to its immense size. It's found near Cuba, Newfoundland and the Atlantic Coast. The blackfin (Parathunnus thynnus) and California's yellowfin (Neothunnus macropterus) run from ten, fifty to one hundred pounds or more. There are several small, localized species of tuna also taken by offshore big game anglers. Here, big rigs, fighting chairs and well-equipped cruisers are necessary for the best sport. Bait is generally trolled squid, menhaden, herring, bonefish or mackerel. Fishing grounds are generally well offshore and the species are not infrequently accompanied by marlin, wahoo and dolphin.

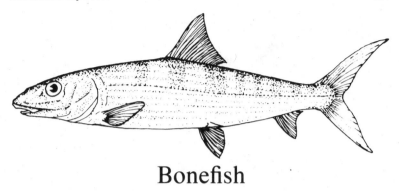

Bonefish

Marlin (Black, White, Striped, Blue)

Commonly referred to as "billfish" because of the long sword preceding it by one-third its length, the marlin is taken well offshore from Cape Cod to South America—in fact, the marlin is taken in most open ocean waters of the world in one species or another. The white marlin (the smallest) ranges in weight from sixty to eighty pounds, while the black marlin tips the scales at well over five hundred pounds. Big game tackle, fighting chair and outrigger fishing cruisers capable of long offshore trips are required. Baits used are bonefish, bluefish, mackerel, ladyfish, mullet and the like. Baits are

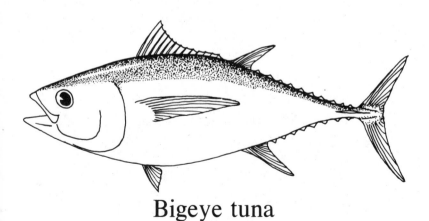

Bigeye tuna

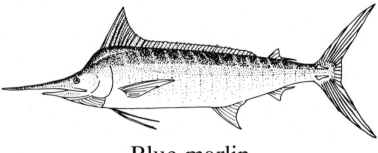

Blue marlin

trolled from outriggers and the angler sits patiently until the skipper's call pierces the dull grinding of the boat engine: "Marlin, marlin sighted on port bow . . ."

Sharks

There are numerous members of the shark family, but only five will be considered here—these are the big ones whose weight and sporting characteristics make them outstanding. The mako (Isurus oxyrhynchus); the white (Carcharodon carcharias); the porkbeagle (Lamma basus); the thresher (Alpias vulpins) and the tiger (Galeo-cerdo cuvier) all have several qualities in common: heavy weight, up to six hundred pounds; insatiable appetites for meat, animal blood

White marlin

Hammerhead shark

and dead fish of any size and description; nasty tempers; terrible teeth and seemingly unbeatable, unending endurance under pressure from the biggest sporting tackle made.

In recent years, more anglers have taken to the specific sport of shark fishing and hence outfitting their boats for real trouble. Gallons of animal blood are poured over the side to form a blood slick on the ocean to attract them. Once hooked, sharks can strain and drain an angler for many hours.

Barracuda and Cobia

Fiercest of all saltwater fish with the exception of the shark, the great barracuda (Sphyraena barracuda) of the Atlantic range in

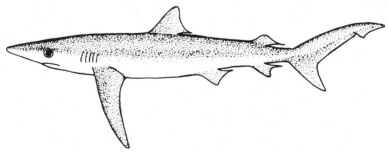

Blue shark

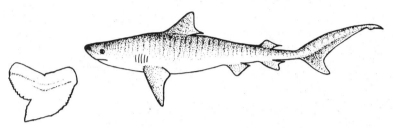

Tiger shark

size from ten to fifty pounds. The Pacific barracuda (Sphyraena argentea) are feared by smaller game and food fish, and have even scared an angler or two by flashing their large, razor-sharp teeth. Both species frequent inshore and beach waters with an occasional visit to the big deep. When taken, it's usually by accident, and most often by big game anglers. Small barracuda are found all season long in southern waters and recently as far north as Cape Cod in the Atlantic. Some prize the meat of the barracuda, but the fierce nature of the fish has held its culinary appeal down. They can be taken in small sizes on conventional light to medium saltwater spinning and boat fishing gear, but the big ones require big game tackle. Their food is anything that moves, including the fisherman.

Thresher shark

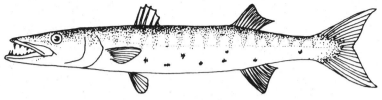

Great barracuda

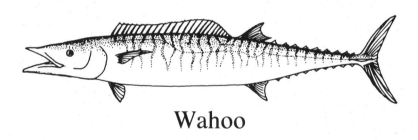

Wahoo

FEMALE   MALE

Dolphin

Wahoo, Dolphin

Not in the least related except for their common grounds, namely, big-deep ocean waters near reefs and drop-offs, the wahoo (Acanthocybium solandei) and the dolphin (Coryphaena hippurus—fish, not the animal variety) range along the southern waters of both coasts all the way to Central America. A big dolphin will weigh from twenty-five to fifty pounds, a wahoo from thirty to sixty pounds. Heavy tackle is needed because they're both rated game fish due to jumping ability and seemingly inexhaustible strength. Baits are similar to those used for marlin and other big game fish: bonefish, mackerel, mullet, menhaden. These baits are trolled on the surface and behind the fishing cruiser.

Glossary

AFLOAT   On the water.

AIRCRAFT CABLE   Special wire designation for leader materials.

ANCHOR   A heavy forging or casting so shaped as to grip the sea bottom and, by means of cable or rope, hold the boat in the desired position.

ANTI-REVERSE   The mechanism on a reel which allows line to be pulled from the reel while the handle remains still.

AQUATIC INSECTS   Those born in stream or lake and which later fly.

BACKLASH   Line rolling over itself backwards due to the reel overspinning.

BAIT CASTING   The casting of plug, lures and baits; a type of tackle.

BAIT FISH   Any species used for baiting larger fish.

BAIT FISHING   Fishing with natural foods rather than artificial.

BALANCED TACKLE   Tackle which balances well in hand and performs to the ultimate, all components including the rod being well-matched to each other such as size and weight of line and reel in relation to terminal rig, lures used, and all ideal for the fish species sought.

BALL SINKER   A round sinker for bottom fishing.

BANK SINKER   Special sinker for bottom fishing.

BASS-BUG ROD   A staunch fly rod heavier than the usual trout weight designed to throw heavy, wind resistant fly rod lures.

BELT BOX   A small metal box for carrying small amount of bait on belt.

BLOOD KNOT   Special knot for attaching hook to line.

BRAIDED WIRE   Leader made from braided strands of wire.

CHART   A map of a body of water containing necessary piloting information.

CLEAT   A piece of wood or metal with projecting ends to which lines are made fast.

CLINCH KNOT   A special fisherman's knot.

COCKPIT   A well or sunken space in the afterdeck of a boat for work or action space.

CREEL   A basket or bag that holds caught fish, most often fashioned of willow or canvas.

DIAMOND SINKER   Diamond-shaped sinker for surf fishing.

DIPSEY SINKER   Sinker with tying ring on top.

DRAG   On reel, adjustable to brake the speed of line flow from the reel spool.

END LOOP KNOT   A knot used to tie a loop.

FIGURE EIGHT KNOT   A special knot for attaching hook to line.

FLAT EYE   The hook eye is flat to hook bend.

FLIES, ARTIFICIAL   Those made to represent insects and bait fish.

FLYING GAFF   A short handled gaff for securing fish.

GAME FISH   Designated fish species known for their gamey fighting qualities and those under conservation law protection.

HAYWIRE TWIST   A special twist to make loop in wire leader.

HOOK EYE   A circular end of the hook to which line is attached.

HULL   The body of a boat or larger vessel.

KIDNEY HARNESS   A wrap around harness for holding large rod.

KNOT   To bend a line. A unit of speed.

LEVEL-WIND MECHANISM   Winds the line back and forth evenly on the reel.

NON-MULTIPLYING REEL   Single-action; one revolution of the handle to one of the spool.

NYLON COATED CABLE   Wire leader covered with nylon.

OFFSET HANDLE   Rod handle angled and designed for better handling of the reel.

PANFISH   Tasty small fish that can be cooked in a pan.

POINT   The sharp point of a hook.

PUSH-BUTTON REEL   A closed-face reel featuring automatic line pickup and release controlled by a push button.

PYRAMID SINKER   Surf casters standard sinker.

SINGLE-ACTION REEL   A non-multiplying reel, usually employed only on fly rods.

SIWASH HOOK   Special West Coast angling hook.

SLEEVE CLAMP   A special clamp to secure loop in wire leader.

SNAP SWIVEL   A swivel featuring a snap for tying on sinkers or other lines and hooks.

SNELL   A hook specially attached to leader material.

SPOON WRAP   A wrap of wire leader for attaching.

SPROAT HOOK   A special hook designation.

STRIKING   Pulling sharply on the line against the hit of a fish in order to set the hook in its mouth.

TAPERED LEADERS   Lengths of almost invisible monofilament material attached between the running line and terminal tackle, tapered down to a relatively fine end.

TAPERED LINES   Lines tapered from thin to thick to thin for balance and casting efficiency.

TERMINAL TACKLE   Various items attached to the end of the line or leader such as swivels, hooks, sinkers, spinners, etc.

TROLLING   A fishing method in which the bait or lure is dragged behind a moving boat.

TROLLING STRIP   Any strip of flesh hooked to lure or plain hook.

ULTRA-LIGHT TACKLE   The lighest and sportiest tackle practicable for the fishing conditions and species to be fished for.

WAKE   The moving waves, track or path formed behind a moving boat. The wakes of larger or faster boats can be very dangerous to small boats in the vicinity.